T0069688

Algerine Spy
in
Pennsylvania

A view of the city of Philadelphia from across the Delaware River drawn by George Heap, under the direction of Nicholas Scull, surveyor general of the Province of Pennsylvania. Engraved by T. Jefferys and published near Charing Cross in 1768. This print includes vignettes of the Battery and the State House as well as a street plan between the Schuylkill and Delaware Rivers. (*Library of Congress*)

The
Algerine Spy
in
Pennsylvania

OR,

LETTERS WRITTEN BY A NATIVE OF *Algiers*
ON THE AFFAIRS OF THE

United States in America,

FROM THE CLOSE OF THE YEAR 1783 TO THE
MEETING OF THE CONVENTION.

—*Facto pius et sceleratus eodem.* Ovid

PETER MARKOE

Edited by
TIMOTHY MARR

WESTHOLME
Yardley

Originally printed and sold by Prichard & Hall, in Market between
Front and Second Streets, Philadelphia, in 1787.

On the title page: —*Facto pus et scleratus codem*, "an act both pious and wicked:" from
line five of Book II of Ovid's *Metamorphosis*. Refers to King Agenor's threat to exile
his son Cadmus if he cannot recover his sister Europa who had been kidnapped by
Zeus. Cadmus fails in his mission but, in his banishment, establishes a new nation
named Boeotia with Thebes as its capital.

Westholme Publishing, LLC
904 Edgewood Road
Yardley, Pennsylvania 19067

Visit our Web site at www.westholmepublishing.com

ISBN: 978-1-59416-063-9
Printed in the United States of America

CONTENTS

INTRODUCTION

Timothy Marr

During the months that the Founding Fathers were meeting secretly behind closed doors in Philadelphia, a packet of letters written by a Muslim spy, Mehemet, was left in darkening twilight outside the office of Philadelphia publisher William Prichard. Included was a letter from an unknown translator explaining that he had received Arabic manuscripts, written over a period of five years, from an anonymous source with a request that they be published for "the good of the United States" (p. 5). The national government was at that time dealing with a protracted hostage crisis during which American sailors languished in captivity in Algiers after attacks by Arabs and Moors that resulted in the capture of their merchant ships. These letters "attracted considerable attention" in 1787 when Prichard published them in *The Algerine Spy in Pennsylvania*, a volume that was advertised up and down the Atlantic coast.[1]

---

1. Joseph Jackson, *Literary Landmarks of Philadelphia* (Philadelphia: David McKay, 1939), 228. The adjective Algerine has since been commonly replaced with Algerian.

This book is one of the earliest, full-length works of fiction published in the United States. It is also the first of several published spy narratives featuring the intercepted letters of imagined Muslims sharing intelligence about the new nation.[2] The letters narrate the story of how Mehemet, in the midst of a secret mission to gather information about the power of the United States, converted to Christianity and gratefully became a Pennsylvania citizen. Mehemet's defection offered readers the hope that the nation's constitutional crisis could be surmounted by expanding the democratic basis of national citizenship. The publication of his intelligence also warned citizens of the dangers of despotism if they were too complacent about protecting their civil liberties. The fact that this book has been out of print and largely inaccessible is the major reason

2. Other Muslim spy narratives include the Mustapha-Rub-a-Dub Keli Khan letters included in Washington Irving, William Irving, and James Kirke Paulding, *Salmagundi* (New York: D. Longworth, 1807); and the Ali Bey letters in Samuel Lorenzo Knapp, *Extracts from a Journal of Travels in North America* (Boston: Thomas Badger, 1818). Discussion of these works as well as a shorter version analyzing *The Algerine Spy* is included in the chapter "Islamicism and Counterdespotism in Early National Cultural Expression," in Timothy Marr, *The Cultural Roots of American Islamicism* (Cambridge: Cambridge University Press, 2006), 20-81. The vogue of imposing classical learning upon a pseudo-Islamic theme can be found in an even earlier American work of fiction that Philip Freneau and Hugh Henry Brackenridge penned as college students in 1770 called *Father Bombo's Pilgrimage to Mecca;* Ed. Michael D. Bell (Princeton: Princeton University Press, 1975).

why only a handful of articles and chapters have inves-
tigated it in any critical depth.[3] This is the first edition
in over 220 years of a rare and interesting book that the
historian Samuel Eliot Morison called "a pungent
satire on American affairs" and Middle East expert
Michael B. Oren chose as one of the five best works
that capture "the long history of America's encounters
with the Arab World."[4]

3. Works of useful criticism on *The Algerine Spy in Pennsylvania* include:
Sister Mary Chrysostom Diebels, "The Prose Satire," *Peter Markoe (1752?-
1792). A Philadelphia Writer* (Washington, DC: The Catholic University of
American Press, 1944), 49-66; Malini Johar Schueller, "Algerian Narrators
in the New World: Washington Irving's *Salmagundi* (1808) and Peter
Markoe's *The Algerine Spy in Pennsylvania* (1787)," *U.S. Orientalisms: Race,
Nation, and Gender in Literature, 1790-1890* (Ann Arbor: University of
Michigan Press, 1998), 67-74; Jennifer Margulis, "Spies, Pirates, and White
Slaves: Encounters with the Algerines in Three Early American Novels,"
The Eighteenth-Century Novel 1 (2001): 1-36; Lotfi Ben Rejeb, "Observing
the Birth of a Nation: The Oriental Spy/Observer Genre and Nation
Making in Early American Literature," in *The United States & the Middle
East: Cultural Encounters.* Eds. Abbas Amanat and Magnus T.
Bernhardsson (New Haven, CT: The Yale Center for International and
Area   Studies,   2002),   253-289
(http://128.36.236.77/workpaper/pdfs/MESV5-9.pdf); Julie R. Voss, "The
United Blessings of Freedom and Christianity": Peter Markoe's *The Algerine
Spy in Pennsylvania," The Eagle and the Crescent: Early U.S. Literary
Encounters with Islam* (unpub. Ph.D Dissertation, University of Kentucky,
2006), 84-111; Allan Christelow, "The Western Mediterranean in an
American Mirror: *The Algerine Spy in Pennsylvania," The Maghreb Review*
31, no. 1-2 (2006): 80-102.

4. Samuel Eliot Morison, *The Oxford History of the American People* (New
York: Oxford University Press, 1965), 291; Michael B. Oren, "Books: Five
Best," *The Wall Street Journal* (June 2, 2007): 8.

The Algerine Spy in Pennsylvania consists of a series of twenty-four fictional letters mostly written by a sixty-year-old named Mehemet during his spy mission to Europe and the United States and sent home to his friend Solyman in Algiers. Both men are members of the court of Osman, the despotic Dey of Algiers, who has assigned Mehemet the "weighty commission" (p. 9) of being the first Algerian to travel to the United States and spy on its strength. Mehemet, because of his candor and experience, is selected to carry out this mission, yet it is one that he could not refuse without being accused of cowardice and treason, and his detractors in North Africa relish having him out of the way. Mehemet acknowledges that during the colonial period "a Pennsylvanian was less known to us, than a Greenlander or a Chinese" (p. 65), but after independence and the successful revolution against Britain, rumors abounded about the extent of American power in the "western continent" (p. 62). Mehemet's assignment is to "separate the specious from the solid" (p. 59) by observing the customs of the new nation first hand and "to inform our illustrious regency of the actual strength of these states, and their future probable exertions" (p. 91).

His journey begins in Gibraltar and Lisbon, and the first ten letters recount Mehemet's experiences in the disguise of a deranged French philosopher "in the midst of infidels" (p. 11). His wide-ranging commen-

tary appraises the global economic affairs of both classical and contemporary political powers, comparing the
policies of Rome and Carthage, as well the eighteenth-
century alliance of Britain and the Netherlands against
France and Spain. He applauds the advantages of trading and internal industry over the imperial economy of
plunder and war. Mehemet not only tolerates but
admires the commercial genius of the transnational
Jewish business community, which is represented by
the contrasting examples of his hosts Solomon
Mendez and Moses d'Acosta, who serve as the inter-
mediaries for the movement of capital and intelligence
between North Africa, Europe, and America. Positing
Islam as the voice of reason in religion, Mehemet crit-
icizes the bigotry and hypocrisy of Christians
(Nazarenes), as well as the absurdities of two rabbis he
encounters. The Algerine also exposes the superstitions
and prejudices of English sailors and derides the per-
verted pleasantries and petty rituals among the British
elite of Gibraltar, especially in his naively humorous
observations of a tea party and a ballroom dance.

Upon his arrival in Pennsylvania in 1783, Mehemet
finds American citizens to be "free, active and intelligent" (p. 58), yet blinded by the hurry of business that
prevents their notice of the "swarthy" (p. 9) spy in their
midst. Inconspicuously taking up residence in an inn or
as a single boarder with private families, Mehemet for-
ays the city on foot "imitating the air and manners of

the people" (p. 66). He spends his days inspecting the peculiar customs of the crowds around him and assessing their institutions, writing about the "partial and incoherent information collected each day" (p. 91). From his position as a foreign observer, Mehemet narrates satirical appraisals of the "tyranny of *fashion*" (p. 69), pointing out the danger of forfeiting natural simplicity for degenerate display. There are letters evoking a Jeffersonian realization that a useful education is the surest foundation for republican government. In another letter he describes a visit to a Quaker Meeting with strange practices so bewildering to him that he believes he is in the midst of a congregation of entranced genies. He writes to his wife Fatima about the coquettish levity of Philadelphia's women, including an account of an enthusiastic female preacher that was based on the real Jemima Wilkinson, who styled herself as an androgynous messiah and also resided in Philadelphia in the mid 1780s.

This work was part of an established genre featuring satirical observations penned by an oriental interloper (perhaps originally modeled on the Greek works of the second-century Assyrian rhetorician Lucian), that emerged in Europe with the publication of Giovanni Marana's *Letters from a Turkish Spy* (who was named Mahmut) in the late seventeenth century. The enormous popularity of these six hundred letters in translation gave rise to two other influential eighteenth-century examples: *The Persian Letters* (1721) by Charles-Louis de Secondat, Baron de Montesquieu, and *The Citizen of the World* (1762) by Oliver Goldsmith. The fictional device of publishing letters that were ostensibly written back to confidants in the East made the homeland into a destination of foreign travel, thereby estranging local customs by licensing fresh perspectives through naïve and impartial eyes. Such works satirized supposedly civilized conventions in ways that humorously fostered broader forms of cosmopolitan critique. Although Markoe's dependence on these European models exemplifies his assertion that American "arts are still in their nonage . . . or cradles" (p. 95), he applies their devices in *The Algerine Spy* to spark in his readers a fuller appreciation of the critical virtues needed to preserve the fragile freedoms that U.S. Americans had newly gained from independence.

The publication of *The Algerine Spy* was in direct response to an ongoing crisis that faced the new republic in its first years. In 1785—only two years after the Treaty of Paris that formally concluded the American Revolution—Algerian corsairs were emboldened by a truce with Spain to sail out of the Straits of Gibraltar. Near where the Atlantic meets the Mediterranean they captured two American trading vessels no longer protected by treaties with Britain. Twenty-one crew members were taken into captivity in Algiers, where some would die of disease, others would be privately ransomed, and ten would languish in captivity for more than a decade. The Dey of Algiers was perhaps influenced to demand a heavy ransom because of America's reputation of successfully defeating the British, its access to the legendary riches of Spanish America, and stipends provided to the captives—reasons the fictional Osman is interested in measuring the actual extent of American power. However, because the weakness of the United States confederation prevented the raising of revenue for ransom, the situation could not be effectively addressed, registering the nation's shameful inability to respond actively to foreign indignities under its first system of government. The capture of these ships and their crew created pervasive paranoia and rumors of transatlantic Algerine depradations that worsened postrevolutionary economic troubles.[5] It is partly for these reasons that the renowned diplomatic historian Thomas A. Bailey could assert that "in an indirect sense, the brutal Dey of Algiers was a Founding Father of the Constitution."[6] Soon after the capture of these ships in 1785, three strangers were detained in Virginia under the suspicion that they might be spies sent from the Dey of Algiers. After an

5. Frank Lambert, *The Barbary Wars: American Independence in the Atlantic World* (New York: Hill and Wang, 2005); Lawrence A. Peskin, "The Lessons of Independence: How the Algerian Crisis Shaped Early American Identity," *Diplomatic History* 28, no. 3 (June 2004): 297-319.

6. Thomas A. Bailey, *A Diplomatic History of the American People*. 10th edition. (Englewood Cliffs, NJ: Prentice Hall, 1980), 65, quoted in Ben Rejeb, 253.

interrogation revealed only some documents in Hebrew, they were deported in 1786.[7] These events register deep American fears that corrupt forces of old world despotism, emboldened both by European desires to subvert the new republic and a Semitic collusion between Jews and Arabs, were conspiring to infiltrate the new republic under the Articles of Confederation.

The anonymous author of *The Algerine Spy* has long been considered to be a Philadelphia writer named Peter Markoe. Markoe was born on the Caribbean island of St. Croix to a wealthy sugar-growing family of Huguenot descent (his last name is derived from the French "Marcou"). In 1767 he enrolled for a classical education at Oxford University and remained in England to complete his legal training at the Inns of Court in 1775. During that time his mother died and his father, Abraham, moved to Philadelphia and remarried an American woman, and later built a elaborate downtown mansion on Market Street. In 1774, Abraham was one of the wealthy founders of the Philadelphia Light Horse, the first volunteer militia established during the American Revolution in which

7. Robert J. Allison, The *Crescent Obscured: The United States and the Muslim World, 1776-1815* (New York: Oxford University Press, 1995), 3-4; Peskin, "Lessons," 299-300. In 1797, Royall Tyler's novel, *The Algerine Captive*, was still disseminating rumors that Jewish/Algerian spies had been sent to the United States and were involved in a conspiracy to inflate the ransom demanded for American captives. *The Algerine Captive.* Ed. Jack B. Moore (Gainesville, FL.: Scholars' Facsimiles & Reprints, 1967), 181.

Peter briefly served as a captain. The Light Horse escorted George Washington on his journey to take charge of the Continental Army in 1775, and its flag, reputedly designed by Abraham Markoe, was the first to feature alternating thirteen stripes representing the patriotic unity of the colonies. In order to protect their properties in the Virgin Islands, the Markoes were required to obey Denmark's official neutrality in the war of independence.

At the conclusion of the revolution in 1783, Peter Markoe moved back to Pennsylvania and became a United States citizen, the same year that Mehemet inaugurated his spy mission in his French disguise. Peter was the eldest son who, neither marrying nor taking up the legal profession, enjoyed instead the democratic conviviality of urban taverns. His trade was his writing but his production was small: he wrote two plays that were never performed (*The Patriot Chief* [1784] and *The Reconciliation* [1790]), and published a number of poems including a collection, as well as authored the anonymous *Algerine Spy,* his only work of prose.[8] At his early death around the age of 40 in 1792, he was known as Peter the Poet, and his obituaries called him "an eminent literary character and an honest man" as a result of his role as a literary spokesman of

---

8. The fullest account of Markoe's life is still Mary Chrysotom Deibels's published dissertation, *Peter Markoe (1752?–1792): A Philadelphia Writer* (Washington, DC: The Catholic University Press, 1944).

the Antifederalist movement.[9] Markoe's French
Huguenot heritage, his Caribbean upbringing with
Danish citizenship, and his British education supplied
him with a breadth of philosophical and ideological
resources. This experience led to a commitment to
American democracy that was more transnational than
most of his fellow members of the Philadelphia mercantile elite, perhaps encouraging him to identify with
the perspective of an alien Algerine outsider.

The appeal for Markoe of Pennsylvania's multicultural democracy helps to explain the centrality of
Pennsylvania in the title of his book. Philadelphia was
the largest city in the United States as well as the political capital of the new nation, with a thriving commercial port that served five states. Pennsylvania's radically
democratic government and ethnic diversity made it a
crucial keystone for prominent political debate over
national constitutional reform. Markoe acknowledged
the weaknesses of the existing confederation of states,
but his politics were allied with the more agrarian par-

9. *Federal Gazette* (Jan. 30, 1792): 3. One obituary noted that he was "frequently styled the *Churchill* of America," referring to the British satirist
Charles Churchill (1731-1764). *Columbian Centinel* 14, no. 45 (February
15, 1792): 179. William Prichard, the publisher of *The Algerine Spy* and
other works by Markoe, acknowledged the poet's merit and honor by writing a poetic eulogy at his death that included these words: "Child of the
muses! truth flow'd from his tongue,/Who virtue taught, and who sublimely
sung;/Who lash'd each vice! A moralist indeed! Bold his satyres, which was
by sense decreed." W. P., "Lines Sacred to the Memory of Mr. Peter
Markoe," *Dunlap's American Daily Advertiser* (February 3, 1792), 3.

the frivolities of Pennsylvania culture. These redemptive virtues are necessary to allow the reader to understand and accept the naturalization of the narrator-spy as a fellow American at the close of the book.

Central to this transformation is also Mehemet's repentance for his misguided use of sexual authority. At the outset of his mission, Mehemet is taken aback by the direct freedoms of the European women he encounters: "Strange, thought I that the man, who, in his harem, inspired awe and even terror, should in his turn, be awed into silence, and shrink from the eye of female observation" (p. 28). Mehemet admired his wife Fatima because she was a woman "with whom silence is wisdom and reserve is virtue" (p. 31). But his power blinds him to the real cause of this reserve. Rather than a sign of respectful love, such "mildness of temper" (p. 120) was her response to the reality that she was his slave and could not resist his advances. With the exception of one letter to Fatima, Mehemet neglects his family and even blames his wife for placing her maternal devotion to their child over her own devotion to him. However, the death of this child extinguishes Fatima's commitment and frees her to express her natural affections for Alvarez, a captive Spaniard who serves as Mehemet's gardener. Together they escape to Europe, where she converts to Catholicism, changes her name to Maria, and embraces legal Christian marriage—a series of acts that seals Mehemet's fate by seemingly confirming his treason to the Dey.

Mehemet's redemption is only complete when he uses the wealth he prudently protected to purchase two farms in Pennsylvania, and offers one to the new couple, promising with paternal charity (and extreme forgiveness) to treat Maria as a daughter. This change in their relationship in Markoe's narrative removes Mehemet's threatening virility (no doubt a reason why the spy is a sexagenarian) as part of the process of transforming him from an advance scout of despotism into a chaste and benevolent American citizen willing to pay reparations for his past misdeeds.

The Algerine Spy in Pennsylvania thus dramatizes how literary expression boldly raised the standards of America's democratic mission and Christian aspirations during a time of political crisis. The book symbolically enacts a multiple conversion through which rational Islam both checks and then bows to Christian truths, despotism dissolves into democracy, and ethnic differences are assimilated into national character. The reform of Mehemet's family and its reconstitution on farms in Pennsylvania becomes a microcosm of the United States as a multicultural and interracial nation. Markoe's *Algerine Spy* recommends the Swiss republic as a model for the United States in ways that correspond with the cultural vision of Jeffersonian agrarianism (whose *Notes on Virginia* was republished by the same press a year after *The Algerine Spy*). Markoe also expands the vision of national incorporation voiced by J. Hector St. John de Crèvecoeur five years earlier in his *Letters from an American Farmer*. Crèvecoeur asserts that in the independent United States "individuals of all races are melted into a new race of man," and this American, "leaving behind him all his ancient prejudices and manners, receives new ones from the new mode of life he has embraced, the new government he obeys, and the new rank he holds."[13] Markoe's work globalizes the terms of this inclusion by naturalizing not only a Spanish Catholic, but also an African who is a former sensualist, infidel, and spy, and a rebellious ex-Algerian female slave (with whom he had pretended to be a husband), as long as they are all willing to adopt American customs and pursue lives of reformed virtue. It is partly for this reason that Mehemet's letters are provided to a translator to be printed "for the good of the United States" (p. 5).

One of the most compelling aspects of this work is the mysterious means by which Markoe makes the letters come to light, even though most readers assumed the author was an American. The disguise of their purported origin is maintained by a complex ruse that they are written in Arabic and other languages, and delivered anonymously to a man only known as S.T.P. with a request that he translate and publish them. That translator himself leaves the letters at the office of the publisher William Prichard "in the dusk of the evening" (p. 1). This device of multiplying the secrecy

---

13. J. Hector St. John de Crèvecoeur, *Letters from an American Farmer* (New York: E. P. Dutton, 1957), 39.

of the spy's revelations enables Markoe and Prichard to conspire together to deliver fresh commentary on the constitutional crisis by capitalizing upon public interest in the Algerine threat. By publishing this intelligence, however, the potential subversion of the spy is effectively exposed. The American press, one of the stays against domestic despotism, regulated the dangers of an uncritical, apathetic, or hypocritical citizenry by reminding its readers of the vigilance necessary to maintain liberty. The public circulation of Mehemet's epistolary reports defuses its subversive espionage, and instead redeploys its intelligence from secret information for the Dey of Algiers to a resource for democratic advancement.[14]

The fact that these multilingual letters addressed to Muslims and Jews are read by Americans in English dramatizes both the democratic power of the press and early national desires for global relevance. Markoe's fiction fantasizes the regulation of threatening difference that the new nation seemed unable to effect in the actual world: the neutralization of the despot, the naturalization of the alien, and the conversion of the infidel. *The Algerine Spy* assured its initial audience that underneath the apparently despotic behavior of threatening aliens there lived incipient democrats who could and would be converted into virtuous Christian citi-

14. See Margulis, 14, 16.

zens. In his last letter Mehemet invokes Pennsylvania to "open thy arms to receive Mehemet the Algerine, who, formerly a Mahometan, and thy foe, has renounced his enmity, his country and his religion, and hopes, protected by thy laws, to enjoy, in the evening of his days, the united blessings of FREEDOM and CHRISTIANITY" (p. 125).

Markoe creates Mehemet's infiltration as an allegory of the need for circumspection and tolerance in the democratic reform of the Articles of Confederation. However, the early ratification of the new Constitution by Pennsylvania's leaders on December 12, 1787 drove Markoe to anger and despair. He remained a disgruntled and dissident Pennsylvanian who was vocal in his minority opposition to centralized national power until his untimely death in 1792. Following *The Algerine Spy*, he penned a poetic Antifederalist lampoon, *The Times*, which was published anonymously in January of 1788. However, Markoe felt compelled to add his name and republish an extended version with Prichard and Hall in July after an Antifederalist petition to repeal the Constitution's ratification was defeated, a development that Markoe found "grievous, unconstitutional, and highly tyrannical."[15] From Markoe's per-

15. Peter Markoe, *The Times, A Poem* (Philadelphia: Prichard and Hall, July 1788), iv. The earlier version of the poem was published in January 1788 by William Spotswood. Also in July, Markoe and Prichard published another satirical stab at the Federalists called "The Storm" which was included in William Falconer, *The Shipwreck* (Philadelphia: Prichard and Hall, July 1788), 107-23.

spective, the new nation had shamefully sacrificed its democratic birthright to appease the ambition and avarice of the elite, effecting the very despotism that Mehemet symbolized by his subversive mission. Markoe has Mehemet wisely acknowledge in one of his letters that "[t]he ambition of princes and the avarice of merchants will never be regulated by systems" (p. 55). *The Times* ends with these lines of unregenerate hope: "*Simplicity* to *Freedom* ever true,/Shall scorn the tyrant or tyrannic few:/On equal rights maintain the People's throne,/And reign with them immutable and *One*."[16]

The United States under the Constitution did in fact pass laws and develop policies that might have prevented Mehemet's naturalization as an American. Mehemet was able to pass in Philadelphia because his masquerade as a Mediterranean man from the south of France helped to explain the darkness of his skin as something other than African. In 1790, the two houses of the National Congress passed the Naturalization Act, which granted citizenship only to "free white persons" of "good moral character." Despite the protest against American sailors held captive in North Africa, and in contrast to Mehemet's narrative of emancipation, the African slave trade to the United States was permitted by the Constitution for twenty more years. In protest of this federal support of slavery, Markoe's

16. Markoe, *The Times*, 35.

unclear political status in the Muslim world. However, Markoe's own limited understanding of North Africa ultimately reflected the insularity of his own supposedly cosmopolitan education. Mehemet's allusions are drawn more from the classical histories of Livy and Plutarch than from familiarity with any Islamic, Arab, or Maghrebi ethos. Indeed Markoe, as did Mehemet in Europe, may have derived some of his cross-cultural knowledge from his encounters with the transnational Jewish community of Philadelphia.[19]

Recent critics of Markoe's work have noted that Mehemet's assimilation through conversion may have imperial undertones. They read *The Algerine Spy* as a founding document that dramatizes how alien others are conscripted from their own cultures to legitimate an exceptional national power.[20] Despite Markoe's own tolerant distrust of centralized authority, his own narrative usurps Mehemet's Algerine voice for nationalist purposes. Markoe invents a Muslim who ultimately apostasizes his religion to become a Christian patriot, trading in the Five Pillars of Islam for the American "pillars of freedom, justice, friendship, and religion" (p. 124).[21] However, it accomplishes this only by excluding

19. Christelow, 90. Christelow's article is the first to attempt to account for the sources from which Markoe acquired his understanding of Algerine politics.

20. Schueller, 68, 72; Voss, 85-6, 109.

21. Voss, 101, n12.

and forgetting Mehemet's Algerine culture. The Tunisian scholar Lotfi ben Rejeb has argued that "Mehemet's Americanization amounts to cultural suicide" at the same time that Markoe celebrates it as deliverance and salvation.[22] Mehemet's Pennsylvania patriotism is constituted on his position as a defecting renegade from his own society and religion, the reverse of the treason that caused disgrace when American captives in North Africa "turned Turk" to survive their ordeals.[23]

The argument that the spy has been fully incorporated into the nation is nevertheless inconclusive because Mehemet himself remains a fugitive at large. As neither the translator nor the publisher claim to have met him, the ultimate provenance of the letters is obscure (even if their actual emergence is a result of a creative collusion between Markoe and Prichard). Did Mehemet make copies of his original letters and supply them to the translator himself? Or could the Gibraltar Jew Solomon Mendez, the recipient of Mehemet's final letter and the intermediary for all of them, be

22. Ben Rejeb, 270-1. See also Christelow, 99 and Margulis, 16.

23. For example, Lewis Heximer converted to Islam and assumed the name Hamet Amerikan. See Jonathan Cowdery, *American Captives in Tripoli.* 2nd. ed. (Boston: Belcher and Armstrong, 1806) in Paul Michel Baepler, *White Slaves, African Masters: An Anthology of American Barbary Captivity Narratives* (Chicago: University of Chicago Press, 1999), 171-2. Cowdery mentions other American renegades who were originally named Prince, Wilson, and West (165, 178, and 180). See also Christelow, 100; Voss, 2.

responsible for their appearance? Questions persist about the limits of Mehemet's national assimilation because he remains in hiding and only stealthily supplies his intelligence for publication. Markoe's fabrication of his Algerine spy thus serves as a creative example of what Mikhail Bakhtin has called "outsidedness," the quality that claims that "our real exterior can be seen and understood only by other people, because they are located outside us in space and because they are others."[24] That Mehemet continues to pass undetected in his new Pennsylvania guise empowers him to live on as a cipher of the revolutionary liberty that Markoe was so devoted to preserving. In his absence he retains the capacity for disclosing more secrets in future communications, ensuring the survival of an outside perspective embodying the virtue of criticism as a central element of faithful citizenship.

The persistence of Mehemet's potential for constructive espionage thus reflects Peter Markoe's experience and frustration as an emergent citizen of the United States. The real author of these letters was himself a naturalized alien who dissented against the emerging dominance of Federalist political culture as well as rejected the materialism of its mercantile ethos. The publication of the letters allows the Algerine spy

24. M. M. Bakhtin, *Speech Genres and Other Late Essays.* Trans. Vern W. McGee (Austin: University of Texas Press, 1986), 7.

to continue circulating within America, symbolizing Peter Markoe's ability to conscript the discriminating intellect itself as an uncensored resource for cultural analysis. Mehemet's surveillance is ultimately transformed from a subversive external threat to the nation to a critical resource of persistent vigilance for its democratic internal maintenance.

The political importance of ongoing domestic criticism is one reason why the prefatory letters by the translator and publisher voice the hope that the unseen Algerine spy will favor them with fellowship and "further communication" (p. 6). Capitalizing on Mehemet's letters as a commercial as well as a critical resource, the bookseller William Prichard humorously solicits readers' comments that will "increase the value of the work by rendering it at once more bulky and amusing" which he promises to add "by way of appendix, to the third or fourth impression" (p. 1). In his poem, *The Times*, Markoe lamented the threats to freedom of the new Constitution (before the Bill of Rights were added in 1791) as a submission to Islamic tyranny: "Whilst the lov'd press no legal bulwarks shield,/And *Christ* in time to *Mahomet* yield."[25] Yet Mehemet's published intelligence in America serves as a bulwark against such a fate. Mehemet writes to Solyman about the social good

25. Markoe, *The Times*, 16.

of circumspection: "the councils of nations, as well as the behavior of individuals, may be benefited by a consciousness of their being narrowly watched!" (p. 66) Prichard compares the "snug little pocket volume" to "an easy good natured friend" (p. 2). willing to go everywhere the reader wishes and prominently displayed the large gilder letters "SPY" on the spine of the book's original bright red leather cover. The first edition of Markoe's book infiltrated Philadelphia with a spirit of humorous critique urging caution at a key moment in the consolidation of national power. May this second edition of the *The Algerine Spy in Pennsylvania* over two centuries later circulate anew as a reminder that critical intelligence and satirical surveillance are still needed to check the excesses of American empire.

* * *

A NOTE ABOUT THE TEXT: This edition contains the complete text of the original and has been reset using modern standard American spelling. No words have been omitted or changed other than their spelling.

THE

ALGERINE SPY

IN

PENNSYLVANIA:

OR,

LETTERS WRITTEN BY A NATIVE
OF *ALGIERS*

ON THE

AFFAIRS

OF THE

United States in America,

FROM THE CLOSE OF THE YEAR 1783 TO THE
MEETING OF THE CONVENTION.

❖❖❖❖❖❖❖❖❖❖❖❖❖❖❖❖❖❖❖❖❖❖❖❖❖❖❖❖❖
————*Facto pius et sceleratus eodem.*
                                    OVID.
❖❖❖❖❖❖❖❖❖❖❖❖❖❖❖❖❖❖❖❖❖❖❖❖❖❖❖❖❖

PHILADELPHIA:

PRINTED AND SOLD BY *PRICHARD & HALL*, IN MAR-
KET BETWEEN FRONT AND SECOND STREETS.

M.DCC.LXXXVII.

Original title page of *The Algerine Spy in Pennsylvania.*

I DO certify, that on this twenty-eighth day of August, one thousand seven hundred and eighty-seven, a book entitled "The Algerine Spy in Pennsylvania or, Letters Written by a Native of Algiers on the Affairs of the United States in America, from the Close of the Year 1783 to the Meeting of the Convention," printed by Prichard and Hall, at Philadelphia, was entered by them in the office of the prothonotary of Philadelphia county as the property of William Prichard.

J B. SMITH, Prothon.

LETTER FROM THE PUBLISHER.

TO THE PUBLIC.

ABOUT a fortnight ago a large packet was dropped in my store in the dusk of the evening, as I suppose. It remained unnoticed till next morning, when, happening to perceive it, I opened it, and, among other written papers, found a letter directed to me, which is subjoined.

In the course of that day and the next, I occasionally dipped into the papers; but as to sell books, not to criticize them, is my business, all I shall say is, that the style, if we consider that the work is but a translation, is tolerably smooth and easy; and the sentiments (due

allowance being made for the disposition and
education of an Algerine) are not unworthy of
the public attention.

As these states abound in critics equal to
any in the world, it may be presumed, that
some of them will condescend to read the
book which they criticize. If these gentlemen
will favor me with their remarks, they shall be
added, by way of appendix, to the third or
fourth impression. This addition will increase
the value of the work, by rendering it at once
more bulky and amusing.

I confess that, although a bookseller, I am
not fond of large volumes. A huge folio has an
imposing air of dignity, which is very apt to
deter people from having any thing to say to it,
as my shelves can testify; but a snug little
pocket volume, neatly bound and lettered, is
like an easy good natured friend, who is ready
to sit down with us near a good fire, or to take
a walk on the commons. If we happen to be
otherwise engaged, we part from the one, or
pocket the other, without trouble or ceremony.

As for the Algerine gentleman, I declare upon the word of a faithful citizen, that I do not know him. If he has ever favored me with his custom, I am highly obliged to him, and, when he gets rid of his melancholy, I shall be happy in presenting him with a copy of the work and a glass of wine into the bargain, which, as he is now a good Christian, I hope he will not refuse.

With respect to the translator—but let him speak for himself—

I am the Public's most

obedient humble servant,

W. P.

LETTER FROM THE TRANSLATOR

WILLIAM PRICHARD.

Sir,

AS the publication of the herewith enclosed letters will probably excite some degree of curiosity concerning MEHEMET, the Spy, I wish it were in my power to gratify it. The letters, written in different languages, but chiefly in Arabic, were delivered into my hands with a note, which contained a request that I should translate and publish them for the good of the United States. They were all without dates, which omission will be excused, when it is considered that they are but copies; but the principal facts mentioned in them are so notorious and recent, that dates seem unnecessary.

Whether they will either instruct or amuse, I will not pretend to say; but I am confident, that they will do no harm. The Algerine spy, although as such inexcusable, is by no means an indecent or immoral writer.

If I were favored with his address, I should express my gratitude to him for his obliging present; and I hope I shall not be deemed to trespass on his bounty by requesting further communication, which, by means of your press, shall be laid before the public.

I am, Sir, with all respect,

Your very humble servant,

S. T. P.

LETTER I.

GIBRALTAR.

WHEN I parted from thee, a train of ideas, at once melancholy and pleasing, took possession of my mind. I was conscious, that I had undertaken an office of the highest consequence to my country and the Musselman faith; that, if successful, I should rank with those, who have gained immortal honor in this world, and the joys of Paradise; that, if unsuccessful, I should suffer disgrace and imprisonment, (death I disregard) pitied by men of sensibility and insulted by fools and knaves. I ingenuously confess, that I was greatly dejected; but was relieved from this anxiety of mind (if relief it could be called) by the most distressing sickness I had ever experienced. My head grew giddy; a nausea succeed-ed; large drops of cold sweat issued from every pore; with difficulty I staggered to my bed, and, clasping my hands, recommended my soul to Allah. I slumbered, as I suppose, about four hours; when, finding myself considerably better, I ventured on deck.

To thee, who, from a very early period of thy life, hast been accustomed to hardships and perils on this turbulent element, this account of my sea-sickness will appear per-fectly ridiculous. If I expected to excite com-passion, I would have addressed this letter to the gallant leader of our warlike troops, or the venerable interpreter of our most holy law. The first has often experienced dangers in the conflict of arms, and the no less perilous intrigues of a court; but I am confident, that his tremors have been greater during a voyage to Constantinople, than when exposed to the roaring cannon or the equally destructive whispers of court-sycophants. The last has never been at sea; but he has often read with exquisite sensibility the description of a voyage by the royal Israelite.

I shall not trouble thee with a minute account of my distresses during the whole voyage; the offensive smell and taste of the water; the roughness of the captain, which I at first mistook for brutality, or the sneers of the sailors, who, having been informed that I was a Frenchman, regarded me with eyes at once expressive of hatred and contempt.

Thou must remember, that when my proposal of embarking for the American continent was accepted, it was suggested to me to appear in the character of a native of the south of France. My knowledge of the French language, the predilection of the citizens of the states for their allies, and the swarthiness of my complexion, induced me to follow this advice. This circumstance exposed me to the insults which I have just mentioned. But the consciousness of the weighty commission, with which I was charged, repressed my resentment. I conversed with them freely in English, which I understand perfectly and speak with tolerable fluency; and very soon conciliated their favor. They partook of my wine, and liberally offered me their grog, which is a mixture of water and a spirituous liquor, highly esteemed by the inhabitants of the new world. The dispensation, which I obtained, permitting me to drink wine, must, I think, include all fermented and even distilled liquors. But as wine only is mentioned, I beg you will consult our great spiritual guide on this occasion, and inform me of his sacred determination.

After a short voyage I landed yesterday in the bay under a promontory,* which with a disdainful superiority, looks down on the ocean, and even its brother Ceuta on the opposite coast. It has been in the possession of the English more than eighty years, who took it from the Spaniards, and, notwithstanding several attacks and sieges, are still masters of it.

Thou may remember with what stupidity both these nations were charged by several of our countrymen during the last war, the one for attacking, the other for defending this use-less rock, as it was rashly termed. But their

---

*Rock of Gibraltar, from the Arabic, *Jebel al-Tariq*. Named for Tariq, the Muslim military commander who took control of Spain in 711 AD. Spain ceded Gibraltar to Great Britain in 1713.

accusations would have ceased, had they considered, that this Pillar of Hercules is no
inconsiderable prop of British opulence and
glory.

I lodge in the house of Solomon Mendez, a
Jewish merchant, to whom I brought letters of
introduction, and shall soon embark for
Lisbon, from which port I shall take passage
for the new world.

Farewell—Be mindful of the man, who in
the midst of infidels will preserve his friendship inviolate. Protect me by thy eloquence
and influence, from the open attacks or insidious machinations of my powerful enemies,
who most probably suggested this enterprise
for the sole purpose of accomplishing my ruin.
Let not the offspring of thy friend experience
the want of a father in his absence; but above
all counsel, assist and console the treasure of
my heart. Assure her that as she has constituted my chief felicity in Africa, no European or
American shall ever rival her in my affection.

FAREWELL.

LETTER II.

GIBRALTAR.

I T may be disputed, whether the possession of this rock has been beneficial to Great Britain. The expense of defending it has been perhaps greater than the commercial advantages derived from it. But it is undoubtedly true, that the Sublime Porte* and its dependencies in the Mediterranean, are highly interested in its continuing under its present masters. No true Spaniard can behold it without indignation, and consequently a wish, that it should be reunited to the kingdom from which it was violently rent, and has been ignominiously retained. It has been, I believe, the principal source of enmity betwixt Spain and Britain, since it was conquered, and has

---

*High Gate (Bab-i Ali), the official name of the Ottoman government in Turkey taken from a gate in the Sultan's palace in Istanbul.

induced the former nation to co-operate with France in all her plans for reducing the power of the latter. Spain, if repossessed of Gibraltar, would probably abate of her attachment to France, to whose views, it must be confessed, she has long been blindly subservient. The loss of that vast tract of country in America, now called the United States, by diminishing the power of Britain in that quarter of the globe, has lessened the terrors, and consequently the enmity of Spain. A new nation has started up in America, which, if actuated by ambition, (and what power has long resisted its impulse) may invade, harass and subjugate several of the Spanish provinces. The enthusiasm of these invaders, the debility of the invaded, the poverty of the states and the wealth of the provinces, will render the conquest of Peru and Mexico by no means difficult. The Bourbon union* already regards the American confederacy with a jealous eye, and will never forgive this new people for having it in their power to attack their possessions in the west, although the temptation may be resisted for a long series of years.

*Political alliance between the kings of France and Spain who were related.

The wars among the Christian powers have generally, I might lay invariably, promoted the interest of the Ottoman empire. Here then is a certain source of animosity, which must advance the splendor and power of the Porte, and may restore thousands of Moorish families to the possession of their estates in the fertile, but neglected provinces of Spain.

You must here permit me to make a short digression in favor of toleration. Had Spain, when she threw off the Moorish yoke, permitted those people to retain their religion, she would still have held the first rank among the powers of Europe. Moderation would have reconciled our forefathers, or, at all events, their immediate offspring, to the superstitions of the Nazarenes.* They were undoubtedly an industrious, as well as a brave and intelligent people. Their expulsion weakened Spain at least as much, as the banishment of the Protestants† reduced the internal resources of France in the reign of Louis the XIVth. I shall

*Qur'anic name for Christians, associated with the town of Nazareth, homeland of Jesus.

†The persecution of the Huguenots by King Louis XIV in 1685 that led to the exile of Markoe's forebears to the Americas.

not attempt a regular dissertation on the fatal effects of religious intolerance; but shall only remind thee, that the followers of Mahomet have been more indulgent to those who profess Christianity, than the different sects of Christians have frequently been to each other.

It must be confessed, that there are schisms even in our holy religion. The disciples of Hali* (not to mention inferior sects) differ in some particulars from the followers of our prophet; but we defy the most virulent Christian to prove, that either the Ottoman or Persian government has racked, burned, or even imprisoned, on a religious account, those who dissent from the established mode of worship in these respective countries. Some brutal Turks and Persians have been known, it is true, to speak insultingly to, and even spit upon, a Christian in the streets. But in all possible cases the dispensers of justice never fail to redress the injury by punishing the aggressor. Here then lies the difference between

---

*Shi'ite Muslims who believe in the Imamate that follows Ali, cousin and son-in-law of the Prophet Muhammad.

Mahometans and Christians in this particular; the rabble among us are sometimes guilty of religious rancor; but in Christian countries, persecution always proceeds from those who are, or at least are supposed to be, the most enlightened. What glory to the generous followers of the bold and intrepid Mahomet! What disgrace to the pretended disciples of the meek and humble Jesus!

FAREWELL.

LETTER III.

GIBRALTAR.

My host, I have already informed thee, is a Jew. Thou wilt consequently suppose him to be guilty of those vices too generally attributed to his degenerate nation. Those of whom thou hast any knowledge, living under a government which despises, insults, and even robs them of the fruits of their industry, are necessarily reserved in their conversation and austere in their domestic concerns. If poor, they are scoffed at by the populace; if rich, they are plundered by their superiors. But in Gibraltar (and I believe throughout the British dominions) they are as fully protected as any other denomination of men. They are, it is true, excluded by law from all the offices of state, nor can they purchase lands. But as their commerce is extensive, their influence is by no means inconsiderable. Their immense property in the national funds gives them a degree of weight equally advantageous to themselves and the public. They are by interest, the strongest of all ties, attached to their country which protects them, and by their correspondence with each other, however widely dispersed, are enabled to collect intelligence of all the designs of foreign cabinets. It may occasion some astonishment, that Britain, which liberally encourages their commercial enterprises, should preclude them from possessing landed property. I will not say, that this prohibition proceeds altogether from wisdom; but I am induced to think, that it has been productive of the happiest consequences. If the Hebrews had been permitted to purchase lands, many of them would have become mere farmers; an useful race of men, I confess, but on a narrow scale, if compared with merchants. The cultivator of the earth in a country not arrived at maturity, is unquestionably the first character, but in a more advanced state of society he must yield to the merchant. In the former state the landholder assists his country simply by his own exertions, or those of his immediate relatives, and may be justly deemed a patriot; in the latter, the merchants by advancing the credit of his nation and often by depressing that of the enemy, by a few strokes of his pen creates fleets and armies, and often without bloodshed ensures success. He is equally a patriot and more of the statesman than the landholder.

Our imagination is highly delighted, when we read the histories of ancient Greece and Rome. We are dazzled by the splendor of their victories, and are apt to attribute more praise to them, than they deserve. But Alexander, at the head of united and victorious Greece, paid the higher tribute to the utility of commerce. If, in the madness of false heroism, he destroyed Tyre, he endeavored to repair the injury by founding Alexandria; and Rome, incapable, by her genius, of commercial greatness, was long retarded in her progress to universal dominion by the policy, wealth and valor of Carthage. Hence this state was entitled to her particular hatred; others she merely conquered and enslaved; but Carthage she utterly destroyed.

It might be entertaining, and perhaps useful, to trace the probable progress of Carthaginian power, if, in the last Punic war, she had subdued her imperious rival. Possessed, at that time, of a very lucrative commerce, she would have aimed at extending it. Conquest would have been but her secondary object. Her daring navigators had already visited all the discovered parts of the world, and had made considerable progress along the coast of Africa, lying on the Atlantic ocean, towards the equator. After a few more attempts, they would have doubled the cape of Good Hope, and the treasures of the east would have rewarded her beneficial industry. That nation, which the silver mines of Spain, at that time the Mexico of Europe, could not corrupt or enervate, would have prosecuted her plan with the genuine spirit of commerce, which encourages a degree of foreign industry, as the reward of superior skill and exertion. Her factories would have increased to cities; these cities, by a happy contagion, would have acquired over the adjacent countries a species of dominion, which, being founded on mutual benefits, would have no less advanced the interests, than conciliated the affection of the original inhabitants. War, as I have said, would have been moderately attended to. Released from the dread of a rival, she would have levied armies and equipped fleets solely to maintain (allow me the expression) the police of the world.

FAREWELL.

LETTER IV.

GIBRALTAR.

I have given thee an imaginary sketch of the probable power of Carthage, (if she had subdued her rival) a name, which ought to be mentioned in the annals of Africa with no less honor than Egypt herself. Let us now review the effects, which the ambition of Rome produced in the human character.

That nation, which boasted its origin from the union of robbers, was necessarily, even in its infancy, incited to war by the hope of plunder. Incapable of industry, and confined within very narrow limits, the Romans could not exist without distressing their neighbors. Having established a place of refuge for malefactors, their numbers rapidly increased by the accession of all the banditti of Italy. Their first chief was supposed to have been the son of Mars.* His actions corresponded with his pretended birth. The murder of his brother inspired his followers with the highest opinion of his hero-ism. Who more fit to reign, said they, than he, who is not restrained by the ties of nature? This sentiment pervaded all their designs, and was infused into their children. It was glorious not only to die for their country, but to assas-sinate their enemies, and even to kill their own offspring.

Thou art sensible, that I am not indulging a romantic fancy. Every page of the earlier part of their history is stained with insidious assas-sination or open murder. A Scaevola* is recorded as a hero, for having thrust into the flames the hand which failed to murder a king at open war with his nation; and a Brutus‡ is exalted to almost divine honors for having

*Romulus, founder of Rome, who slew his brother Remus.

†"Left-Hand," the name given to the Roman noble Gaius Mucius who thrust his right hand into the fire to protest the invading Etruscan king in an legendary episode from Livy's *History of Rome*.

‡Lucius Junius Brutus, the founder of the Roman Republic, who executed his sons Titus and Tiberius for failing their military duties as told by Plutarch.

condemned to die two of his sons, whom the laws of his country might have banished without his unnatural intervention.

But thou wilt say, that the Romans were, at the period I allude to, emerging from barbarism; that great souls, unenlightened by sound philosophy and true religion, are necessarily guilty or excesses. That they were barbarians at this period, is granted; but let me ask thee, at what time were they enlightened? Their kings, with the sole exception of Numa*, were the worthy leaders of the greatest desperados we read of. Their perpetual wars in Italy (I might have called them massacres) ought to have united the whole world against them, as the pests of human nature.

Nor can we attribute their ferocious exploits to the examples of their kings. After the regal authority was abolished, their ambition was insatiable. Italy soon became too narrow a space for their cruelty and thirst of false glory. Having repelled Pyrrhus†, who had brought

*Numa Pompilius, the legendary Sabine chosed as the second King of Rome, celebrated for his wisdom and piety in Livy and Plutarch.

†Pyrrhus of Epirus, a great Greek military commander who fought against the Romans in the third century BCE and became the King of Sicily.

succors to his allies, the Tarentines, they attacked Sicily, at that time allied with Carthage. This war routed the Carthaginians, who being hitherto chiefly employed in commercial pursuits, or engaged in war as an inferior object, could not behold the encroachments and usurpations of the Romans without feeling a just resentment. They armed, they fought; and after experiencing triumphs as well as defeats were exterminated by their ungenerous rivals.

Thus fell Carthage, the emporium of commerce, the nursery of humanity! And to implacable was the fury of her conquerors, or so destructive have been the ravages of time, that the works of her artists, and the writings of her poets, statesmen and philosophers are no where to be found, except the comedies of Terence* and the Periplous of Hanno.†

Perhaps I have heightened this picture from a predilection for a people, who were the ornament of Africa, and masters of the place of my

*Roman playwright Publius Terentius Afer who was taken from Carthage as a slave; author of the famous quote "I am a human, nothing that is human is strange to me."

†A manuscript of the Carthaginian King Hanno describing an expedition along the west coast of Africa in the fifth century BCE.

nativity; but I am of opinion, that every impartial person who reviews the Roman history with the eye of philosophy, must execrate the insidious policy and unbounded ambition of that restless and domineering people.

FAREWELL.

LETTER V.

GIBRALTAR.

ALTHOUGH comfortably lodged, I am impatient to enter on my office; but am doubtful, whether I shall take passage from some port in France for America, or from Lisbon. In the meantime my host, to whom alone the object of my travels is known, endeavors to render my abode in this place as agreeable as possible. He has introduced me to all his acquaintances, some of whom are men of letters; the rest are merchants. His wife, although sufficiently domesticated, partakes of all the amusements of the place; the visits, and is visited by, several respectable families. In deportment an Algerine, a Frenchman in dress and language, I was at first the object of their amazement; but after the second visit it abated, and I am no longer the theme of their whispers. Accustomed to women who are reserved, bashful and timid, I at first blushed when spoken to and answered their questions with diffidence and hesitation. Strange, thought I that the man, who, in his harem, inspired awe and even terror, should in his turn, be awed into silence, and shrink from the eye of female observation! But I soon suppressed these unmanly feelings, and entered into the spirit of their conversation, which was decent and lively.

Thou wilt probably be amused with an account of our conversation. We were seated in a large room, which was rendered as cool as possible by a free admission of air; but the ladies, whose constitutions, I presume, were more susceptible of heat, than those of the men, kept fanning themselves perpetually, complaining, at every pause in the conversation, of the intense heat of the weather. They frequently rose from their seats with seeming hurry, and, stepping hastily to a mirror, adjusted their neck-dresses with the greatest composure. Their conversation was as unguarded, as their looks and motions. They spoke of their absent friends without reserve, and sometimes with acrimony; that a matron was anxious to be divorced from her husband, and that a virgin was eager to elope with her lover. I heard with astonishment more than three female voices at a time. A discourse directed to one lady, was interrupted by another, and the half-uttered question was mutilated by the premature answer. A lapdog occasionally attracted their notice, which, by turns, they fondled, kissed and even spoke to with all the rapture of maternal tenderness.

This scene, which, if related to me, I should scarcely have believed, was interrupted by a man, superbly, but fancifully dressed, bearing in both hands an oblong japanned machine, on which several beautiful vessels were arranged, filled with a smoking liquid. Imagining him to be one of the guests, I rose from my feet and bowed to him according to the Nazarene fashion. A roar of laughter proceeded from the females, and even gentlemen could scarcely abstain from smiling, while a blush of sensibility overspread the cheek of the attendant, for such I now discovered him to be. He presented the japanned utensil to each of the company in turn, who took hold of a species of plate which supported the vessel, filled with the hot liquor. This was sipped by all the company with evident marks of satisfaction, although but a few minutes before they had all complained of the intense heat of the weather. Having attentively observed the ceremonial, I was not at a loss how to act. But as the attendant approached me, his blushes were renewed and the laugh was repeated, although not so obstreperously as at first. Just at this instant a boy entered in great agitation, and whispered his business in the ear of a lady, who was observed immediately to turn pale. A dozen essence-bottles were instantly applied to her nostrils, and as many fans were in motion. I was truly distressed for the lady, but what was my surprise, when I was informed, that her fainting was occasioned by a misfortune, which had happened to her monkey, who, in attempting to climb a tree, had fallen and slipped his shoulder. She sighed, wept and wrung her hands, while tears of sympathy trickled down the check of these tender hearted ladies. At length the fair mourner, supported by two of her particular friends, was conducted to an inner apartment in all the dignity of sorrow. I embraced this opportunity of retiring to my apartment, by no means edified by a company where the absent had been maligned, a stranger insulted, and a dog caressed; and where more sorrow had been lavished on a monkey, than would have been felt for an expiring child.

How different, my friend, are these women from the beloved of my soul; who is more intent to hear, than eager to speak; who, satisfied with my love, aims not at the admiration of others; with whom silence is wisdom and reserve is virtue!

FAREWELL.

LETTER VI.

GIBRALTAR.

As soon as the company had retired, my friend entered my apartment, and informed me with great delicacy, that the awkwardness of my deportment had induced the gentlemen to make very particular enquiries concerning me; that he had however satisfied their curiosity by informing them, that I was a French gentleman, addicted to study and fond of retirement; that in some of the letters, which I brought with me, hints were given him of an apprehended derangement in my intellects, to prevent which, traveling had been prescribed by my physicians; but that, for his part, he believed I was only a philosopher. I thanked him for this explanation of my behavior, and am determined to improve upon the idea in my travels.

At supper I was introduced to a Rabbi, highly esteemed for his probity and admired for his learning. In the course of our conversation, I discovered, that he entertained a very exalted opinion of his own understanding, and was by no means willing, that his abilities should be overlooked by others. The disgust, occasioned by the tender hearted ladies, was now worn off, and I felt myself disposed to relish absurdities of another nature.

I happened to mention, that the present age was greatly indebted to ancient Greece for literature and science, and bestowed some encomiums on Aristotle. At the name of this celebrated philosopher I observed the cheek of the Rabbi to glow with indignation. "That Aristotle, cried he, has enlightened the world, I readily acknowledge; but it is well known from whom he derived his learning. He attended his pupil, Alexander the Great, in his conquest of the East, and after the taking of Jerusalem, was entrusted with the writings of

Solomon and the rest of our sages, which the Levites had preserved in the temple. From these volumes he extracted that mass of knowledge, which he published as his own, and then destroyed the originals." This instance of national pride reminded me of a story, pretended to be believed in the West; that an apostate Monk and a profligate Jew composed the sacred al-Koran,* which our illustrious prophet promulgated for the benefit of the elect. How confirmed in error must that infidel be, who can utter so improbable a fiction?

The Jews are, I think, the principal merchants in Gibraltar; but may it not be asked, in what part of the world, where they are on a footing with the rest of the inhabitants, are they not the most industrious and wealthy part of the community? Wholly employed in commerce, they always educate their children for the mercantile profession. We rarely find young persons among them, who aim at applause by a contemptible display of unnecessary literature or superficial science. Yet there

*Orientalist legend about how the Prophet Muhammad composed the Qur'an with the assistance of a Nestorian Christian named Sergius or Bahira and/or a Jew named Abdullah Salim.

are among them men, whole genius and acquirements might entitle them to seats in the first academies of the world. As prudence is their characteristic, they are more solid than shining. They are no longer the object of religious fury. Even Spain is become tolerant, and Portugal has ceased to be barbarous. The descendant of Jacob can now find an abode in every civilized country, and, as long as he obeys the laws, may bid defiance to rapacity and bigotry.

It may be reasonably supposed, that the genius of the Hebrews, which for ages has been oppressed by the rude hand of fanaticism, will now spread and flourish anew. Every nation, which protects them, is entitled to their exertions. But while they promote the good of the country where they reside, by a beneficial commerce, they ought not to neglect those arts, which, by adorning, improve human nature. Agriculture is ready to reward their industry a hundred fold; their lutes and harps need not continue hung on willows;* edifices, although inferior to Solomon's palace,

*See Psalm 137.

may give mankind an idea of their former skill in architecture; they may range through nature from the hyssop† to the cedar; and while they wait the coming of their Messiah, they may render themselves worthy of his presence, by charity and benevolence.

May the light, which shone from Mecca, irradiate the minds of these infidels, and guide them into the paths of truth!

FAREWELL.

†A fragrant spice from a hardy shrub; the phrase hyssop to cedar measures the extent of Solomon's natural wisdom from the least to the greatest, see 1 Kings 4:34.

LETTER VII.

GIBRALTAR.

M Y host is very desirous of giving me an insight into the manners and amusements of the Nazarenes, that they may not appear altogether strange to me on my arrival in the new world. He is fully acquainted with the object of my travels, and will doubtless be secret, because it is his interest to be so. To have attempted an enterprise of this nature, without imparting the secret to at least two foreigners, would have been little short of madness. Although an economist by nature and habit, I may require more money than the sum I shall take with me. To draw bills in the new states on a merchant at Algiers would expose me to inevitable destruction, either from their government or the populace. I have therefore settled a mode of correspondence with Solomon Mendez at this place, and shall make similar arrangements at Lisbon with Moses d'Acosta.

It may be asked, as I travel in the character of a French gentleman, why I have not established a correspondence with some mercantile house in France? To this I answer, that, although it is right, for many reasons, to assume the character of a Frenchman, I think it highly dangerous to entrust my secret with any of that nation. An affected or real attachment to these new republicans, the hope of conciliating their favor, or the dread of his own government, might induce a Frenchman to betray me. Even the vanity of being the subject of public discourse might stimulate him to my ruin. But from Jews I apprehend no manner of danger. They will not betray me from either patriotism or vanity. Their immediate interest will prompt them to be faithful, and they have much to hope from my future patronage in Algiers.

I might immediately proceed through a part of Spain to Lisbon; but I shall be less exposed to discovery by taking passage in an English vessel. The mariners of that nation are rough and unsuspicious. When they hear I am a Frenchman, they will conclude they know the worst of me.

I had written thus far, when I was invited down stairs to partake of the amusements of a ball. I accepted the invitation for two reasons. I am supposed to be a Frenchman; and a refusal might have brought my country into question. I am going to the American states; it is therefore necessary that I should be as much acquainted as possible with the English fashions.

On my entering the room, I made a low bow (a circumstance I am careful never to forget) and seated myself in a chair, which separated two matrons, whose respectable countenances challenged that veneration, which from their dress and behavior they seemed unwilling to claim. The hot liquid, which is called tea, was handed round in the manner, which I have already described. They drank it, because, I presume, they were cold; and they fanned themselves immediately afterwards, because, I am confident, they were hot. The contest betwixt the tea and the fan continued for some time. At length the tea retired, and the fan, which had received great assistance from the handkerchief, remained master of the field. The musicians now entered, and, having neglected to tune their instruments before their admission, reminded me of the discordant harmony mentioned by one of the Roman poets.* But this was probably done from the view of rendering by the contrast their music doubly agreeable. The instruments being now ready, I looked round with some impatience for the dancing girls, who, I supposed, were ready in the next room. In the mean time, a young gentleman, approaching with a hat in his hand, made me a low bow. I thought, I could do no less than make him another. He bowed again, and proceeded to another gentleman, who, after giving and receiving a bow, took the hat, and walking with becoming

---

*Quid velit et posit rerum Concordia discors, or "What the discordant harmony of circumstances would and could effect." Horace Epistles (I, 12, 19).

gravity towards one of the matrons, between whom I was seated, bowed to her. To convince the company, that she was both young and active, she rose from her seat with such agility, that her ascending bosom and his descending nose were almost in contact. The gentleman threw back his right leg, and, drawing his left leg towards it, bowed most profoundly, his eyes very modestly fixed on the ground during a few seconds. The lady with an air of complacency and dignity looking full in his face, and, placing both her hands on her waist before, gently threw back her left foot, and, in a manner, which I cannot describe, seemed sinking beneath the level of the floor; then rising gracefully to her natural height, she tendered him one of her hands, which he gently received with one of his. He now conducted her towards a door, which opened into another apartment. I at first imagined they were going to enter it; but both suddenly turning, he bowed, and she sunk and rose again. The music now began, and the lady expanded the lower part of her apparel in a manner to me altogether new and astonishing. After a very short space, he bowed and she sunk again, then both turning half round, the bowing and sinking was repeated. The gentleman with his right hand now took hold of the lady's left hand, (consequently only one half of her garments remained expanded) and both of them, moving slowly and majestically, advanced towards the middle of the room, when, describing nearly a semicircle, they retreated in opposite directions. The lady's left hand, being now at liberty, restored her garment to its full expansion. They continued in motion about two or three minutes, approaching, crossing and retreating, when the lady, extending and waving her right hand in a most bewitching manner, the gentleman also extended and waved his; and they advanced towards each other, till the tips of their fingers met. Then retreating and again advancing, their left hands performed the same graceful ceremony. They continued approaching, crossing and retreating about two minutes longer, when the lady, with a languishing look, letting her garment drop into its natural position, extended both her arms, and advanced to meet the gen-

tleman, who with his arms also extended,
approached her with more than usual brisk-
ness. After turning round, they repaired to the
spot, where the ceremony began, from which,
after three more sinks and as many bows, the
gentleman lead her to her seat; and after one
more bow and a concluding sink retired.

This serious mummery concluded, I imagined the dancing girls, according to the
Algerine fashion, would be now introduced;
but, to my great astonishment, it was repeated
by almost all the company. A pause of about
ten minutes succeeded, when the ladies, having quitted their seats, began to adjust their
dresses, which I could not perceive had been
discomposed; their fans were not neglected
and their handkerchiefs were well employed.
After some consultation, attended with many
bows and sinks, the males and females formed
two distinct rows, each male opposite to a
female at about the distance of three feet.
Hitherto their countenances had been settled
and even severe, their conversation carried on
in whispers, and their demeanor more expres-

sive of devotion than festivity; nay, I had been almost tempted to believe, that they had been engaged in performing some religious ceremonies, not unlike the rites of the ancient Corybantes,* or the ecstatic evolutions of our holy dervishes. But how was I deceived!—One of the musicians stamping with his foot by way of signal, the sprightliest notes were heard. In an instant gravity was put to flight, and in my opinion, decorum suffered not a little. Smiling, capering and nodding ensued. A gentleman turned a lady round with one hand, then with the other, sometimes three turned round together, sometimes four, and, occasionally, even six. The circle appeared to me their favorite figure; but, to prevent giddiness as I suppose, they sometimes practiced the right line. One figure gave me much satisfaction, which, after some observation, I discovered to be the arithmetical 8.

Thus far they proceeded on mathematical principles; but in the course of their fooleries, I thought I perceived a degree of mystic

*Priests of the Phrygian goddess Cybele who engaged in ecstatic sacred rites.

morality. The lady at times fled from the gentleman, as if she was offended; while, he, from
the hope of appeasing her anger, followed her
with becoming tenderness; but deeming her
implacable, and conscious of his own dignity,
gives over the pursuit and flies from her. She,
justly apprehensive of losing him entirely, follows him in turn; a reconciliation ensues, and
their hands are reunited. It was altogether the
most diverting scene I had ever beheld, and I
had every reason to be pleased, that no hired
dancing girls had been introduced. The ladies
and gentlemen, some few inadvertencies
(which ought not to be mentioned) and one or
two slips, (attended with no bad consequences) excepted, performed their parts with
grace and agility, and, as I was the sole specta-
tor, were entitled to my warmest applause.

I have as yet received no letters from
Algiers; but, should any arrive at this place
after my departure, they will be dispatched to
Lisbon by Solomon Mendez. An English vessel, in which I have already engaged my passage, will sail in a few days for that celebrated

port. Thou wilt doubtless give me a particular account of all that has been done or is doing at court or in the city. If Fatima's grief has subsided, she will inform me of my domestic concerns. I have invested her with sufficient authority for the government of my harem; but in dubious cases she will apply to thee for advice. Her beauty at first inflamed my heart; her discretion, I am certain, will secure my esteem.

FAREWELL.

LETTER VIII.

LISBON.

I am induced to think that sea-sickness resembles the small pox, with which we are never afflicted a second time; but I speak with becoming dissidence, not choosing to build an hypothesis on a single fact.

My voyage from Gibraltar to this beautiful port was in every respect delightful. The winds were favorable and gentle, the sea as smooth as I could have wished, and the azure of the sky seldom obscured by a cloud. I found myself so much at ease, that I was almost constantly on the deck.

Doubtless, thought I, if the sea was never agitated by tempests, a considerable part of mankind would prefer it for their abode; like the Chinese and Hollanders who, with their families, reside on rivers in floating mansions. Several occupations might be followed as well on the sea as the land. Raw materials, supplied by the cultivator of the earth, might be manufactured by the inhabitants of the ocean. A tariff, regulating the commerce of the terraqueous globe, might easily be established; fish might be bartered for flesh and vegetables; and, since the ladies on both elements must have ornaments, pearls might be exchanged for diamonds; nor would the powers of the earth have any reasonable excuse for waging war, as long as any part of the ocean remained uncolonized. Archimedes* asserted, that, if he had but a spot to stand upon, he would play at tennis with the ball which we inhabit; for the establishment of my system, I require but the annihilation of tempests. Nor should the sea-scurvy be mentioned as an objection by the medical faculty, till the plague is eradicated by their skill; the latter disorder being at least as destructive as the former.

---

*Greek mathematician who said ""Give me a place to stand on, and I will move the Earth."

Before we passed the rock of Lisbon, I observed a particular archness in the looks of the sailors, which gave me no uneasiness, as I was acquainted with the cause of it. My friend, Solomon Mendez, had informed me of a custom among English mariners, of exacting a tribute from all on board on their first seeing this celebrated rock. I readily complied with an usage which, like many others as pertinaciously adhered to, has no foundation in nature or reason. The wine was produced; the sailors wished me health with a surly benevolence, and we jovially entered this noble port, which for several years was the center of commerce between Europe and Asia.

Thou art not unacquainted with the exertion of maritime enterprise and military prowess, which distinguished this people in the fifteenth century. The secrecy with which they conducted their plan of deposing King Philip, their prudence in choosing the Duke of Braganza* for their monarch, their conquests in Asia, and their settlements in Africa and America, contributed to render them a rich

*Since 1640, the title of the male heir to the throne of Portugal.

and a glorious nation. They may even at present be considered as a people possessed of a considerable share of commerce; but their national valor is no longer the theme of panegyric.

The mere historian is capable of giving us a regular detail of events. It belongs to the philosopher alone to trace the rise and fall of national character, and to investigate those causes, which exalt men to heroism, or sink them in servitude. I confess myself unequal to the task, but shall only remark, that the revolution in Portugal was simply a change of masters. Don Juan was certainly a brave and humane prince; but the royal authority, on the deposition of Philip, was in no respect restrained or regulated. Thus their political happiness depending on the characters of their succeeding princes, the Portuguese have shared the fate of other nations in similar circumstances; they have been wisely governed.

It has been my fate, since I left Algiers, to travel with Englishmen and sojourn with Jews. I am lodged at the house of Isaac d'Acosta, whose civility makes ample amends for his extreme bigotry. Methinks I hear thee exclaim, are not bigotry and civility incompatible? By no means; a wolf subdued by his keeper, is a harmless animal in his presence; and this Jew, not entirely recovered from the dread of the inquisition, is a tractable being.

May the great inquisition of reason be established throughout the world! Thus shall our holy faith be established in the hearts of the barbarous idolater, and the obstinate Jew and Christian!

FAREWELL.

LETTER IX.

LISBON.

THE Hebrew religion being odious to the people and obnoxious to the government, my host is but little troubled with the company of the Portuguese. Nor is his disposition or talents suited to liberal conversation. To me he is distant; to his family morose. How different from Solomon Mendez, whose house was the abode of cheerfulness! I am impatient to begin my voyage, confident, that I shall find more society on the Atlantic than in this populous city. But let me not be hasty or unjust. Perhaps his reserve is the result of constitution; or his affairs may be deranged; or his domestic felicity impaired. He has probably been rendered unhappy by a disobedient child or a false friend. In short, I am willing to assign any reason for his supercilious distance, rather than attribute it to a bad disposition.

Yesterday after dinner I had some conversation with a Rabbi, who is in appearance less arrogant, than his brother at Gibraltar, but more base and wicked. As a specimen of his conversation, I shall relate a tale, which he told. "When God created Adam, said the Rabbi, he formed him so high and large, that his head reached the heavens, and his sides extended from the east to the west. The angels, terrified at his appearance, implored the protection of the Creator, who, to rid them of their fears, put his hand on the head of Adam and reduced his size to one thousand cubits; but, according to other Jewish doctors, to less. His first wife was called Lileth, who, being formed of as good earth as himself, disdained to submit to his authority, and flying up into the air, refused to return to her husband, although entreated by hosts of angels." From this improbable fiction he inferred the extreme degeneracy of man, and the inherent obstinacy of woman. At the conclusion of this legend, equally improbable and absurd, Isaac nodded assent; but his family discovered evident marks of dissatisfaction. I wanted no further proof of the baseness of this sanctified villain, who aimed at ingratiating himself with his patron by destroying his peace of mind. The cause of his discontent was now evident. A domestic traitor embittered his life, and established in his bosom that worst of inquisitions, a distrust of his own family.

I shall certainly disclose my sentiments to d'Acosta on this head before my departure, my conscience otherwise will not be at rest.

As my stay will be short, I shall not have it in my power to give thee an adequate idea of this city, which I am told, is as well built, as it was before the earthquake. Portugal is not my object. Her weakness is too well known at Algiers to create apprehensions. Ignorance, sloth and barbarism characterize her sons, and her daughters are the victims of pride and superstition. Her streets swarm with monks, and her convents are crowded with nuns. Too

eager in the pursuit of commerce, she neglected agriculture and manufactures. Her gold,
which enriches others, is dross to her, and the
precious stones of the Brazils can scarcely pro-
cure bread for her children. Yet this country
was not always contemptible. Her people were
once industrious, and her priests were learned.
She could boast a Camoens and a Gama,* and
was governed by an Emanuel† and a
Braganza; whose names are at this day less
known in Portugal, than in any other part of
Europe. Surely this nation was ordained to
accumulate wealth to reward the industry of
the English and the valor of the Algerines!

A philosophical history of commerce,
would be an invaluable present to mankind.
But if ever it should appear, I will venture to
predict, that its principles will be but little
attended to. The ambition of princes and the
avarice of merchants will never be restrained
or regulated by systems. The custom-house
books alone will be read by the former. If the
imports have been productive, nothing further

---

*Luís Vaz de Camões: famous 16th-century Portuguese poet; Vasco da
Gama: explorer and discoverer of the sea route to the East Indies in 1498.
†Manuel I, 14th King of Portugal who reigned from 1469-1521.

will be required. The merchant, in summing up his accounts, will be perfectly content, if there be a considerable balance in his favor; but experience evinces, that Britain, has derived more solid wealth from the tin mines of Cornwall, than Spain from the silver mines of Mexico; and the nutmegs of Borneo have been more beneficial to Holland, than the diamonds of Brazil to Portugal.

FAREWELL.

LETTER X.

LISBON.

THE ship, in which I have engaged a passage, will sail for the new world tomorrow. I shall soon behold a region, which has never been trod by an Algerine. A mixture of hope and fear, of delight and terror, occupies my heart; but religion and patriotism support me in the conflict. I consider myself as another Empedocles.* Anxious to explore the causes of those conversations, which agitate Ætna and lay waste the fair fields of Sicily with liquid fire, he perished in the glorious attempt. My fate may be similar; but my glory shall be greater. He died without accomplishing his

---

*Empedocles: a Greek philosopher from the 5th century BC who died by throwing himself into the active volcano Aetna on the island of Sicily in an attempt to be viewed as immortal; however, when the lava cast back one of his bronze sandals, his wish was foiled.

object; but if I arrive in the new states, which have lately been the political Ætna of the world, I shall seize every opportunity of acquiring and communicating information.

A vast field lies before me. An extensive coast, abounding in harbors; an immense tract of country, divided into thirteen states, but united, with respect to national exertion, under one head; a soil, capable of producing all the necessaries, and most of the luxuries of life, the greater part of which is still covered with the noblest timber, and abounds in the most useful mines, the inexhaustible materials of future navies; towns rising into cities, and cities already aspiring to be the emporiums of commerce; the inhabitants free, active and intelligent; their governments mild and enlightened; religion promoted by a benevolent toleration, and morality enforced by the brightest examples; these blessings have been founded throughout Europe, as eminently possessed by the new states. The echo has reached Algiers and attracted the attention of her vigilant regency.

But as in all matters of consequence, vague conjectures are indulged and hasty conclusions are drawn; as facts are often exaggerated by fancy, or misrepresented by interest; as truth has been too frequently violated by enthusiasm, and philosophy itself has been the dupe of hypothesis, it was thought necessary to employ a man of observation and experience, who, by residing on the spot, might separate the specious from the solid, and, divested of prejudice, be directed solely by candor. After many consultations, the eyes of our governors were fixed on me. My friends imputed to me the necessary qualifications, and my enemies in silence expressed their approbation. I accepted the office with affected joy; for had I hesitated but a moment, my courage and my patriotism would have been questioned; and the malice of my enemies would have been as effectually gratified by my disgrace at home, as it can be by want of success abroad. The former was inevitable, the latter is but probable.

All letters of consequence from me shall be sent under cover to Solomon Mendez at

Gibraltar, who will take care to forward them to Algiers. All letters directed to me from Algiers must also come through his hands.

Having now arranged our mode of correspondence, I must trespass on your patience with respect to my private concerns. I received from the treasury the day before I sailed, two thousand Johanneses* for the purpose of defraying my expenses, with assurance of a reward adequate to my trouble and risk. A part of this sum I have deposited in the hands of Solomon Mendez; the remainder I take with me, together with a sum belonging to myself.

No man of prudence ought to defer the disposal of his affairs till the hour of sickness. My will therefore, which I delivered, properly executed, to thee, will convince Fatima that I have not been unmindful of her attachment and fidelity; the rest of my property, (some few marks of my esteem excepted) is settled on my child. The younger part of my slaves I have emancipated; the rest will not only have freedom, but competency; I owe no money, and all

*Portuguese gold coins.

that I could claim from others, was either received or compounded before I sailed; so that this executorship, if I should die, will be attended with as little trouble as possible.

Perhaps what I have just written will appear to thee to be the result of timidity. But wilt thou rashly conclude, that I want courage, because I am prudent? Once for all, let me tell thee, that I go prepared to execute my commission, with a mind as unruffled, as when under thy command I assisted in repelling the enemies of our faith and country. I anticipate the honors, which our government shall bestow on me; I hear the shouts of applauding thousands; I grasp the hand of congratulating friendship; I am clasped in the folds of exulting love—farewell—let Fatima know—but, enough—

FAREWELL.

LETTER XI.

TO THE SAME.

PHILADELPHIA.

I am arrived. I tread on the western continent. A native of Algiers is lodged under the roof of a Pennsylvanian. Yet the genius of the state seems unconscious of danger, and the unsuspecting crowd are as busily employed in their affairs or pleasures, as if I was at home extended on my sofa. So let them be. Released from the fatigues and perils of war, let their young men indulge in dissipation, and their maidens in festivity; let their farmers resume their long neglected ploughs, while their merchants anticipate their ideal thousands. I am pleased with their bustle. The more they are occupied, the less notice will they take of me. The mind, which is eager in the pursuit of wealth or pleasure seldom stops short to indulge curiosity. The cloud, which prevented the Carthaginians from perceiving Æneas and Achates,* those illustrious spies, was undoubtedly the hurry of business.

I have delivered my letters of introduction to the gentlemen to whom they are addressed. These letters describe me as a French gentleman, who wishes to see the country before he engages in either commerce or agriculture. Some hints are given of a domestic misfortune, which has rendered his own country disagreeable to him. I decline dining abroad, but in the afternoon occasionally visit a few families. As it is known that I came last from Lisbon, no French letters could be expected from me. I am yet at an inn, which is crowded with foreigners, but shall remove shortly to lodgings in a private family, which admits but one stranger. The few Frenchmen whom I have seen, finding me distant, are determined to be equally so. Their pride in this particular is far from being disagreeable to me.

---

*In Virgil's *Aeneid*, Venus veiled these two men with a cloud to enable them to approach Carthage without being seen.

A part of my money is deposited in a bank, which in its principles resembles many of the European banks; but as I am not thoroughly acquainted with its plan, I shall not entrust it with all my stock.

You cannot as yet expect any thing particular from me. In general I am pleased with the appearance of the people. Their deportment is gentle and unassuming, and my ears have not as yet been offended with many oaths.

I observe a particular class of men, their hair loose and unpowdered, their hats uncocked, their linen without ruffles, and their coats, which are generally light colored, with mohair buttons. Can these be the officers and soldiers of the late army, who, having parted with their military dress, still affect an uniformity in apparel? I am convinced I am right; and I think I perceive in them a commanding look and an air of dignity, which are more readily acquired in camps than cities.

I was called to this employment so suddenly, that I had not time to read many books

written on American subjects. The British
colonies on this continent were as little known
to the Algerines before the last war, as the
most remote parts of Europe and Asia. We
had often heard of Peru and Mexico through
the medium of Spain; but a Pennsylvanian was
less known to us, than a Greenlander or a
Chinese. They shall however have no reason in
future to complain of our neglect. Due attention shall be paid by us to their national
ensigns on the ocean; nor shall their government or resources continue unnoticed. They
have invited all the mercantile world to their
ports. Our countrymen, more modest than
others, shall visit only their coasts. Several
nations have complimented them with splendid embassies. Averse to magnificence and
ostentation I live among them without ceremony, and shall not flatter their pride or excite
their avarice by promises of commercial
treaties never intended to be performed. If my
employment was known, it is probable that I
should be condemned to die by their tribunals,
unless torn in pieces by the populace. How
ungrateful, how ungenerous would such con-

duct be, since it can be proved, that the councils of nations, as well as the behavior of individuals, may be benefited by a consciousness of their being narrowly watched!

I spend a part of the day in walking through the city, partly to preserve my health, and partly to imitate the air and manners of the people. My head is perfectly reconciled to my hat, and my instep, which at first was sorely oppressed, cheerfully submits to the tyranny of the buckle. My body, which was at first rendered almost incapable of action by my Lisbon tailor, performs its evolutions, according to the discipline of the country, with ease and agility, and at my meals I handle my arms with sufficient dexterity. How dull must the Russians have been, who spent a century in attaining accomplishments, which I have acquired in a few weeks. But as vanity is dangerous and offensive, I suppress its emotions.

When I survey my person in a mirror, I rejoice for two reasons; first, that I resemble a Christian, and secondly, that I am not observed by an Algerine. I have so much the air of a Christian slave on his first landing at Algiers, that if Fatima were to see me in this dress, I should risk the loss of her affection.

FAREWELL.

LETTER XII.

TO THE SAME.

PHILADELPHIA.

THESE Philadelphians seem to me as well calculated to excel in commerce as to triumph in war. Their river is crowded with shipping, and their warehouses and shops with merchandise. Almost every man I meet is or seems to be a merchant. I am frequently jostled in the street; but how can I be offended, since I as frequently jostle others. Even the pride of a Castilian (if a Castilian could condescend to mix with traders) would not be offended at their well meaning bustle. But as I have nothing to sell, and want to buy but a few trifling articles, I shall not expose myself a second time to the risk of suffocation in a place, which they call the City Coffee-house.

It is surprising to see the immense quantities of rich manufactures imported into a country, which, as I am informed, has no silver mines or any other rare production of nature. These importations, I am led to think, can only injure the country by introducing a premature luxury with its concomitant evils.

In most nations there are three sorts of tyranny; the first civil; the second ecclesiastical; the third I shall call the tyranny of *fashion*. The first is well known in Algiers; the second has been heard of; but the third is altogether unknown. The Pennsylvanians have known but little of the first, and nothing of the second; but the greater part of them is grievously oppressed by the last.

The origin of *fashion* is perhaps coeval with the creation of man; but the more enlightened are of opinion, that, immediately after the fall, she sprang from the head of Eve, as Minerva is said to have issued from the brain of Jupiter. At first simple and artless, she indulged herself in innocent levities. She formed a head-dress of flowers for Eve, and another of green leaves for Adam. But the father of mankind, with becoming dignity, rejected the present, till, persuaded by Eve, he consented to wear it to screen him, as he said, from the too powerful rays of the sun. After this success the influence of fashion extended to their sons and daughters. Her invention grew more lively and her exertions more varied. In these days, it is recorded, she was attended by simplicity, a nymph whose cheeks vied in freshness with the blushes of the morn, and whose limbs, frequently exercised in the chase, excelled in symmetry and strength. Guided by simplicity the reign of fashion was gentle and delightful. The maidens, obeying her dictates, were lovely and tender; and the young men, who were then under the dominion of *reason*, were sincere and affectionate. The fragrant fields, the delicious fruits and the transparent streams, constituted the luxuries of man, while the harmony of the soul was improved by the music of the groves.

But as happiness, since the great transgression, has been inconstant and fleeting, a gradual degeneracy took place. The young men became thoughtless, irregular and dissipated. Rejecting reason and disdaining the guidance of simplicity, many of them were seduced by the siren voluptuousness; others pursued the phantom false glory, and not a few were infatuated by the demon avarice. The maidens finding the young men growing inattentive to their charms, and determined at all events on exciting admiration, were, with much reluctance, compelled to dismiss simplicity and call in art to the assistance of fashion. By this alliance fashion was at first strengthened; but afterwards weakened. The maidens, it is true, triumphed in the contest, but soon abused their victory. Many of them, by the advice of art, formed a league with levity and caprice, and some of them have gone so far as to set humanity at defiance, and are closely allied to deceit and cruelty. It is difficult to say, how this unnatural warfare will end; but it is very probably, that, unless matters are speedily compromised by fair concessions, the young men will have recourse to insensibility and neglect, and the young women will yield to peevishness and despair.

FAREWELL.

LETTER XIII.

PHILADELPHIA.

I have seen the building, which they call the University; but know nothing of its regulations. A worthy citizen lately told me, in the joy of his heart, that boys are well instructed in it on the English plan, and at a pretty cheap rate.

I am truly astonished, that the wisdom of the state has not established a system of education adapted to its constitution and government. Are they not aware, that the education of youth ought to be particularly attended to in republics? I am convinced, they are. Their good sense is unquestionable; but they appear to me too much attached to the customs of the old continent.

In the universities of Europe, as I have been well informed, great pains are taken to render the students as useless as possible to themselves, their families and their countries. What benefits can be derived from societies, where, after much misspent application and an irreparable loss of time, a young man is imperfectly instructed in two or three unnecessary languages; where reason is fettered by logical rules, and religion involved in metaphysical subtleties, and where the mind, too often disgusted by unsuitable studies, loses all relish for either elegant literature or useful science. Boys, even in their infancy, are too often designed for a particular profession by their parents or friends. This is evidently absurd, inasmuch as neither their talents or inclinations can he consulted at so early a period. But the absurdity is enhanced, when the youth, destined to the mercantile profession, must pursue those studies, which as he advances in life, he will find altogether useless and scarcely ornamental, and which are only calculated to render the lawyer a wrangling sophist, and the divine an artful polemic. Would any man in his senses apprentice his son to a tailor, when he intends him to be a shoemaker?

When I know more of their plan of education, I shall inform thee more fully on that head, and shall only observe at present, that the most powerful operations of nature are performed in the simplest manner. The soil, the shower and the sun, are sufficient to produce the towering oak, as well as the humble shrub.

FAREWELL.

LETTER XIV.

PHILADELPHIA.

THE legislative authority of this state is lodged in a single house, elected by the people, and is called the Assembly. The executive power, elected also by the people, is lodged in a Council. The president of the council is appointed by the joint ballot of the assembly and council. The judicial authority is separate from both. Every seventh year a Council of Censors* is elected by the people, who are authorized to point out all violations of the constitution, and in short all state misconduct. This council has also the right of calling a con-

---

*As stipulated by the 1776 Pennsylvania State Constitution, two members of every town and county were elected every seven years to evaluate the activities of the government and to recommend any necessary censure, impeachment, or repeal, including calling a convention to amend the Constitution.

vention, who are empowered to explain and amend the constitution. This short sketch may give thee some idea of this republic.

The constitution, which seems to have been dictated by wisdom, has been greatly censured by some political writers. Their grand objection appears to be, that as the legislative authority is lodged in a single house, there can be no balance. Even if this be granted, to what will it amount? As the house can never be unanimous in any serious attempt on the rights of their constituents, the minority will always operate as a check, till the people are alarmed. I am greatly mistaken, if this check will not be adequate to the danger; if not, what can be said, but that the people have been weighed in a balance, and found altogether light and unworthy of political freedom. In short, no form of republican government can long oppress a brave and enlightened people. If their constitution is experimentally found to be good, they will maintain it; but the best will prove defective, if they are ignorant of their rights, or inattentive to the preservation of them.

Men of lively imaginations are fond of similes. The constitution of Pennsylvania, says one, is like a loaded wagon and he fairly proves the resemblance. A good constitution, says another, is like a pair of scales—and he also establishes his simile.

When I was a lad I was thought to possess a tolerable knack of making similes. In middle aged men fancy begins to flag; however I will try my hand.

The superiority of a single legislature is thus proved.—

FIRST PROOF.

The constitution of Pennsylvania may be compared to a foot-ball, which is kicked from goal to goal by two parties or sets of players, with alternate triumph. The spectators are deeply interested in the success of the one or the other party. Well kicked, says one; there it goes, cries a second; here it comes, exclaims a third; what a fall neighbor Bustle has had, roars a fourth; he is up again, like a clever fellow, bellows a fifth. Huzza! Huzza!—But, if a second foot-ball should be introduced, the greatest confusion would ensue. Two footballs at once! What a solecism in that manly exercise!

SECOND PROOF.

The constitution of Pennsylvania may be compared to a piece of beef transfixed by a spit, and placed horizontally before a rousing fire. The spit (and with it the beef) is turned round regularly by an ingenious piece of mechanism called a jack, which is proved, by daily experience, to be equal to the task. But should a speculative cook introduce a second jack, which should attempt to govern the other end of the spit, who can affirm, that this innovation would be productive of any solid advantage? On the contrary, would not this second jack be at once an expensive and useless article, not to mention Betty's extraordinary trouble in winding up two jacks, and her mistress's loss of temper in finding the dinner every day either too much or too little done.

THIRD PROOF.

The constitution of Pennsylvania may be compared to a hen's egg, (a found one, I mean;

an addled egg will not suit my purpose) placed between two hands, the fingers of which are intermixed with each other. The ends of the egg being equally pressed by the hands, the egg will continue unbroken, although the greatest strength should be exerted. But should another egg be placed in contact with the first, the least pressure would infallibly crush both; and thus the hands would be in a filthy condition.

In a republic parties must exist; perhaps you will say I have already caught the infection; but I sincerely hope, it will not be imputed to partiality, that I adduce but one simile in confirmation of the opposite opinion.

The constitution of Pennsylvania is like a wheel-barrow. That state has but one legislature, and a wheel-barrow but one wheel.— Good—Now if this wheel-barrow be managed carelessly or rashly (and those who direct wheel-barrows are as liable to neglect and inadvertency, as those who superintend states) it will most probably be overturned, and its contents discharged into the kennel; whereas if a double wheeled wheel-barrow had been provided, it would not have been by half exposed to so much danger; but your marketing most probably would have been brought in safety to your door.

While these infidels are disputing about government, may thou continue an ornament to thy country, and a terror to a corrupted populace, whose vices, if they were ruled by even the mildest laws, would merit the severest punishments!

FAREWELL.

LETTER XV.

TO FATIMA.

PHILADELPHIA.

Two of thy letters are now before me. Why wilt thou tear my heart with thy tender complaints? Art thou not always present to me? Thrice every day I address myself to Allah to comfort thee in my absence.

Even this absence, which thou called cruel and intolerable, ought to endear me to thee. To render myself worthy of thy charms, thy tenderness, and thy virtue, I defied the terrors of the raging ocean, and have ventured to breathe the same air with profane Christians. But my rewards, though slow, will more than compensate my toils and dangers. Algiers will acknowledge my services, and Fatima will again bless me with her love.

Our child, thou say, is sickly. Thy maternal care may be excessive. Fatima, remember, that thy child, however dear, has no right to rob me of thy health.

In Pennsylvania enthusiasm is frequently found; but the influence of superstition is trifling. I have lately heard the rhapsody of a female preacher.* I figure to myself thy extreme surprise on this occasion. Yes, Fatima, a female preacher, in a garb, long, white and flowing, her head uncovered, her hair in natural ringlets, her countenance by turns expressive of pity and anger, of joy and terror, proclaimed to an attentive audience the coming of Christ. Yet she is not supposed to be mad. Although women are forbidden by one of the first Nazarene teachers† to speak in their churches, or to appear in them with their heads uncovered, yet this woman, in violation of both these precepts, dared to appear in the

*Jemima Wilkinson was a mystic evangelical who called herself the Universal Public Friend. She began to visit Quaker groups in Philadelphia in 1782 where her claim to the return of "Christ in Female Form" led to an incident of public stoning.

†The Apostle Paul, "Let your women keep silence in the churches: for it is not permitted unto them to speak; but they are commanded to be under obedience, as also saith the law." 1 Corinthians 14:34.

manner I have described. She was not only listened to attentively, but even excited tears.
Fatima, this woman, thus appareled, or, to
speak more properly, almost unappareled,
preached to a crowded congregation in a civilized country.

What shall I tell thee of a city, where
women appear barefaced in the streets, and,
what is still more extraordinary, the men
behold them with insensibility. I saw this very
morning a man in decent apparel accost a
well-dressed woman; grasping her ready hand,
he led her across the street, and she thanked
him with a smile, to which no man but her
husband could be entitled. Even in the
churches they gaze on the men with undaunt-
ed eyes, nor have I, since my arrival, seen a
blush on a female cheek, a child about ten
years old excepted, who walking carelessly had
been in danger of falling. When the cheek
ceases to blush, the heart, I conclude, is grown
callous to shame. Yet are they lovely in the
extreme. Nature has profusely adorned them
with charms, but a bad education diminishes

the luster of their beauties. They often speak before they are spoken to; they smile in the presence of men, and a giddy girl, the other day, not more than sixteen, at the tea-table, the room full of company and in the sight and hearing of her venerable parents, laughed immoderately at the distress of a young gentleman who had scalded his lips in sipping his tea somewhat hastily. She threw herself backward in her chair, then forward, and continued agitated by convulsive laughter more than two minutes, her cheeks glowing, her eyes darting fire, and her bosom rising and falling during this paroxysm of outrageous mirth. At length rising hastily and tripping light as a wood-nymph, she darted out of the room, and retired up stairs. After a short absence she returned to the company with a countenance, as composed, as if she had been guilty of no indiscretion.

If this young woman were blest with thy conversation, how would thy precepts and example at once enlighten her understanding and improve her conduct! She would learn from thee, that not even the beauty of a Houri* can atone for the levity of laughter.

FAREWELL.

*A beautiful virgin in paradise promised in the Qur'an to the true believer.

LETTER XVI.

TO — AT ALGIERS.

PHILADELPHIA.

THE attention paid to the body of a deceased friend in this city is decent and amiable; but the manner to a stranger must appear particular and ludicrous.

A man is employed to announce the death of a citizen. For this purpose he raps at all the doors, and in a loud and solemn tone of voice invites the family to the funeral. I went yesterday to purchase a pair of gloves at a shop, the mistress of which is pregnant. While I was busied in trying them on, a trumpeter of death, thrusting his funereal face into the shop, pronounced the doleful invitation in shrill and tremulous accents. The woman turned pale and had scarcely strength to call for a glass of water. Mentioning this affair in company, I was told, with an air of indifference, that the woman must have had weak nerves and was probably a stranger.

In one of my late walks, I perceived a number of these men, whom in a former letter I conjectured to be the officers of the late army, entering the door of a large building. Finding that they were followed by several not dressed in uniforms, I took the liberty of entering with them. I perceived a great number of them seated on benches, placed at equal distances with great exactness. I sat down among them, prepared, if questioned, to have told them, with the greatest politeness, that I was a French gentleman on my travels, and would be extremely happy in being honored with their acquaintance; but not one of them took the least notice of me or of each other. Their ladies, who seemed also to wear uniforms, were seated separate from the men. An awful silence prevailed, which I had hitherto imagined was not numbered among Christian virtues, especially when ladies are present. At length the men began occasionally to groan, and the women to sigh. An air of serious sorrow was diffused over all their faces, which (with shame I confess it) affected me with horror. Not a word was uttered; but the sighs and groans were repeated with scarce any intermission. Surely, thought I, this is a scene of enchantment. For what purpose are there people assembled? mirth cannot be their object; for they are all serious, and some even sorrowful, nor can mercantile business be transacted in such profound silence. Have they committed excesses during the war, which they publicly meet to expiate? This cannot be the case; for their humanity was as conspicuous as their valor; besides, with what cruelties can their wives and daughters be charged, who seem equally sorrowful and penitent? A thought now prevailed in my mind, which I am ashamed to confess even to thee. I suspected, that I was seated among some of those benevolent Genii, whole marvelous exploits are the subjects of our romances. Impressed with this idea, and determined on being convinced, I trod, as if by accident on the toes of my next neighbor. The young man withdrew his foot somewhat nastily and looked as if he felt pain; but continued as silent as before. He is composed of flesh and blood, thought I with much satisfaction, and doubtless their females, many of whom were pretty, are equally so.

At length I concluded, that they were assembled to see and hear one of those exhibitions (I think they are called tragedies) with which the Nazarenes are extremely delighted, because they make them weep; but that the performers had disappointed them.

The whole assembly, as if a signal had been given, rose at once from their seats, and quitted the house; and I repaired to my lodgings, ruminating on the strangest scene I had ever beheld.

FAREWELL.

LETTER XVII.

PHILADELPHIA.

THE object of my voyage to this continent, was to inform our illustrious regency of the actual strength of these states, and their future probable exertions; of the manners and pursuits of the inhabitants; their commerce, manufactures and agriculture; their government and laws.

Confident that the substance of my letters will be more attended to than their style, and that little method can be expected from a man, who commits to paper partial and incoherent information collected each day; I continue with cheerfulness to execute my commission, not doubting, that due allowance will be made by my illustrious masters for the weakness and incapacity of their slave.

The strength of these states does not consist in numerous and disciplined armies, or well appointed fleets. When his country demands his service, every citizen is a soldier. The army, which repelled the British forces, it is true, exists no more, except a few companies sufficient to check the inroads of the Indians; but their militia in the midst of peace is preserved in decent discipline. The people being free and their enemies remote, there is no occasion for a standing army.

The last war has convinced these states of two serious truths; they are too strong to be conquered, and too weak to think of conquering others.

Although an Algerine, devoted to the service of my country, you must permit me at times to be the philosopher—at least in words. There can be no excuse for one nation making war on another, but the want of sustenance. This people if but moderately industrious, will not for ages make use of this plea. Their soil is productive and their climate not unfavorable; nor is their population by any means proportioned to their extent of territory.

Their governments are censured by several among themselves. These censures are the strongest proofs of the excellence of their governments, since no man is punished for his censures. Were an Algerine supposed to have imagined only in a dream what a Pennsylvanian speaks, prints, publishes, maintains and glories in, he would suffer the severest tortures.

The manners and behavior of the people correspond with their government. No man creates or feels terror. The national countenance is therefore mild, and the national deportment manly. There are undoubtedly some unworthy citizens; but the noblest soil often nourishes the most venomous serpents.

Of their private virtues I can only say, that benevolence must prevail among a people, who build hospitals and never inquire about a man's religion.

The Pennsylvanians, said an exiled foreigner to me, are inhospitable.

They have given thee a country, said I.

They want the graces, said a sop.

But they are modest, said I, and capable of improvement.

They do not, said a dancing master, sufficiently encourage merit.

A worthy blacksmith, whispered I, with whom I have some acquaintance, will give thee employment.

Their women are distant, and insensible, said a coxcomb.

They are fully apprised of thy merit, said I.

Yet it must be confessed, that the trading part of the community is discontented. By excessive importations the manufactures have been greatly injured, and the merchant begins to think, that commerce on a small scale would have been more advantageous, than the wild plan, which has been pursued. As soon as the war was over, the American republics seemed to have inconsiderately adopted the commercial plan* of Holland. That commonwealth, superabounding in men, wisely encouraged commerce. Situated in the center of Europe, her ships supplied one nation with the produce and manufactures of another. She even established colonies in Asia and America. Her councils at home were wise and steady, and her triumphs abroad were at once brilliant and solid. Her heroes protected her merchants, and her merchants honored and rewarded her heroes.

The American states are in a very different situation. The number of inhabitants bears no proportion to the extent of their country. The arts are still in their nonage, and many of them in their cradles. Why therefore did her statesmen borrow maxims from rich and triumphant Holland, when Switzerland, laborious and frugal, could have furnished them with better.

*In the late eighteenth century, Switzerland was idealized by many writers as a republican refuge of liberty amid the monarchies of Europe.

May I venture to say, that there is a taste in government as well as the polite arts. Inattentive to the want of proportion and symmetry, we are too often captivated by the brilliancy of the colors.

FAREWELL.

LETTER XVIII.

TO THE SAME.

PHILADELPHIA.

I have given thee a hasty sketch of the constitution of Pennsylvania, and intend shortly to acquaint thee with the system, which constitutes her a member of a confederation, consisting of thirteen states represented by a Congress.

The constitution of this congress, which assisted by patriotism, was found adequate to the exigencies of war, is discovered to be defective in peace; like a ship, which having resisted the fury of the storm, is endangered by the hollow swell during a calm.

A Convention consisting of members from all the states, is expected to meet in this city

for the purpose of revising the confederation.*
It is expected, that their resolves will silence all
disputes by remedying every grievance. For my
part I doubt the success of their deliberations,
although sanctioned by the presence and
enlightened by the wisdom of their late commander in chief.

General Washington, who has done as
much as any hero, and a great deal more than
most, who have been flattered with that title,
resides, as a private gentleman, on his estate in
Virginia. Those who are honored with his
conversation, are delighted with his affability,
vivacity and solid sense. In the field he has
manifested the qualities of the general and the
hero; at his abode he displays the accomplishments of the gentleman, and the virtues of the
husband and friend. But the most arduous task
remains; the talents of the legislator are now
expected from him.

During the heat of the war the confederation was formed by the noblest efforts of patriotism and wisdom. But patriotism was some-

*The Constitutional Convention met in Philadelphia from May 25 to
September 17, 1787, indicating that Markoe may have penned at least some
of Mehemet's letters in the spring of that year.

times more active than judicious; and wisdom often saw defects, which she could not remedy.

The state of Rhode Island, the least considerable in the union, has hitherto defeated the best commercial plans.* She has refused to send members to this convention, and by this conduct will defeat unanimity, and countenance defection and revolt.

The state of Massachusetts Bay is now convulsed by the desperation of factious individuals; but the wiser part of the community happens to constitute a majority. Some blood however has been shed, and more is apprehended. In Massachusetts Bay, an ignorant multitude, headed by Shays,† have attempted—they know not what; but in Rhode Island the opposition to federal measures is conducted by the government, the members of which are guided by their private interest which they perfectly understand.

---

*Rhode Island vetoed the impost of tariffs in 1781 preventing the ability of the government under the Articles of Confederation to collect needed tax revenue.

†Daniel Shays led an army of indebted rebellious farmers in 1785–86 against the Massachusetts state government in an attempt to prevent its Supreme Court from acting in support of creditor demands.

As interest is generally a more prevailing rule of action than justice or patriotism, it is highly probable that Rhode Island will persevere in her opposition; and compulsive measures, should they be adopted by the other states, will but excite resentment and provoke resistance.

Ever attentive to the welfare and glory of my country, I have revolved in my mind the means of rendering this very probable revolt beneficial to Algiers, and glorious to the Sublime Porte, by establishing an Ottoman Malta* on the coasts of America. An European Bonneval† was received, honored and promoted by the ministers of the Porte. Is not an American Shays entitled to equal rewards, if capable of rendering equal services? Should this idea merit your approbation, I will immediately (but with due caution) commence a negotiation with Shays, the Massachusetts insurgents, and the refractory

*This strategic island in the Mediterranean Sea, located between Sicily and North Africa, was owned by an order of Christian Knights who had successfully resisted a siege by the forces of the Ottoman Sultan in 1565.

†Claude Alexandre, Comte de Bonneval was a French military officer who moved to Turkey in 1729 and, as a convert to Islam with the name Humbaracı Ahmet Pasa, commanded Turkish artillery forces against Austria and Russia.

leaders of the revolt in Rhode Island. They will without doubt expect a large sum of money, in which, I think, they ought to be gratified. But the gold, for greater security, must be conveyed to their ports by a very respectable fleet, and presented to their leaders by a Bashaw of Three Tails* at the head of about one hundred thousand spahis and janizaries.† This army, acting only on the defensive, will effectually protect them from the resentment of their late associates; and, as all nations ought to pay for protection, these new subjects may be permitted to pay their tribute to the sultan in a certain number of virgins.

The dominion of the island being thus secured, free ports must be established for the Algerine vessels, whose cruises, it is true, will not be rewarded by the capture of many American vessels, (the navigation of the states being almost totally ruined by disunion and faction) but their defenseless coasts, bays and rivers may be plundered without the least risk,

*A high official in the Turkish government appointed by the Sultan and signified by horse tails displayed on a standard carried before the leader.

†Cavalry and infantry recruits in the Turkish army.

and their young men and maidens triumphantly carried into captivity.

The resentment of an offended noble subjected Spain to the yoke of our forefathers for ages. May not this mad insurgent, in order to gratify his pride and satiate his resentment, involve his country in similar evils?

FAREWELL.

LETTER XIX.

PHILADELPHIA.

THE republican form of government is extremely flattering to the pride of man. Orators, poets and philosophers, have founded its praises, while the civilized part of the world has listened with rapture. Who is not soothed by the splendid dreams of Plato and Rousseau? Who is not roused by the thunder of Demosthenes and Cicero?

But in all matters, which involve the welfare of nations, fancy should be restrained and judgment alone consulted.

In every form of government the people are undeniably the source of authority. The throne of the greatest despot, as well as the tribunal of the humblest magistrate, is founded on the consent of the governed. I may be told, that despotism is generally established and always maintained by *force*. But can the personal force of one man control and subdue a nation? Alas! the depravity of thousands must co-operate with the ambition of their leader, and the power of the supreme tyrant is supported by inferior tyrants for the gratification of their own passions.

I have often lamented the situation of our Deys. No sooner is one murdered, than another is elected by the murderers of his predecessor. Should he dare to decline this honor, his refusal is followed by instant death. To preserve his own life, he is obliged to act the tyrant, and reluctantly consents to murders, which the brutal soldiers demand and execute with rapture. The authority of the Dey is founded on the soldiery—and surely the soldiers are men.

Has not Constantinople herself often beheld an emperor triumphant in the morning and a headless trunk at night, while his trembling successor is compelled by the janizaries to accept the semblance of authority, as a sanction for their rapine and cruelty? Let no man call him a monarch, who is every hour exposed to the sabre of a popular janizary. The shrine of the faint may be gazed on; but the offerings are the property of the priests. But I may be told, that these are the excesses of a ferocious soldiery.—Are not these soldiers men?

Let us now visit Russia, the most extensive monarchy in Europe. A woman*, without any natural right, has been raised to the throne of that country by the soldiery, who by this single act govern the monarchy and the monarch. She takes care to supply them with pay and plunder, and they continue to respect the work of their own hands. Here one part of the people (all could not be present at the election) chose a sovereign for the whole, and for fashion sake are content to be called subjects. Therefore the authority of this autocratix is derived from the people.

*Catherine II, known as Catherine the Great, who served as queen of Russia from her coronation in 1762 until her death in 1796.

The French monarchy shows great attention to the nobility and soldiery; and for very good reasons. The soldiery and nobility support the crown; and are not nobles and soldiers men? If not, what are they?

The last monarchy I shall mention is Sweden. The illustrious monarch of this country, the worthy nephew of the immortal Frederick (and he too derived his authority from the people, who were constantly represented by two or three hundred thousand delegates, elected with great caution and fully instructed in the principles of government) this king of the Goths, I say, resenting that one part of his people should be oppressed by another, formed a wise resolution, that there should be no longer any complaints on that head. Assembling therefore both parties, he by the advice of proper counselors, chosen from the body of the people, brought the contending parties to reason. The rights of both nobles and people were placed in his hands, and he seems determined to keep them as pledges of their affection. Surely all must confess that his authority also is derived from the people.

It can be proved, I think, (without citing any more examples) that all human authority and power are derived from the people; because, I apprehend, that, if there was no people, there could be no human authority or power.

What minion of despotism, after seriously perusing these arguments and examples, will deny that authority proceeds from the people? Or what enthusiastic demagogue, who is capable of conviction, will insist, that dominion not only proceeds from, but is inherent in, the people? The first ought to reflect, that there can be no stream without a source; and the second must be convinced by observation, that rivers invariably seek the ocean. There is occasionally a partial reflux of power, but it never reaches the fountain head.

FAREWELL.

LETTER XX.

PHILADELPHIA.

I am pleased that thou hast received in good condition the map of these states. It will show thee at one view the amazing extent of the country. The rivers are numerous and deep; the harbors capacious and secure, the cultivated land is generally extremely productive, and the soil, which is still covered by forests, planted by the hand of nature, promises equal fertility.

Their constitutions, formed by a great majority of the people, inculcate as much liberty as men in society can enjoy. New laws, when necessary, are made by delegates freely chosen, and administered by officers, who glory in being deemed the servants of the public. The people, temperate and laborious, seem only to want encouragement, which may excite emulation, and systems, which may direct their their exertions. The phantom of foreign commerce, no longer pursued with inordinate avidity, must soon yield to the solid efforts of domestic industry, guided by the wisdom of the philosopher and patriot. If this encouragement is given and these systems established, the American republics will no longer be tributary to European industry, and the speculations of our Algerine statesmen will be found altogether ideal and illusive.

I expect with impatience permission from the regency to return, which I beg you will solicit with all the ardor of friendship. My domestic concerns may require my immediate presence, and claim all my attention, especially as in this station I can render no essential service to my country. What refinements of policy can be apprehended from popular assemblies, who are more studious to increase the happiness of the people than to create enemies? Their ambition ought not to be dreaded by foreign powers; nor should their factions invite fees, since, on the first appearance of hostilities, they would undoubtedly unite in repelling invasion. Even the unworthy conduct of Rhode Island will not stimulate the other states to oppress or desert an unenlightened or unprincipled sister, nor could the Porte derive any advantage from the possession of that island. Its wealth would not pay, nor its territory feed, a sufficient garrison; nor would the annoyance of the trade of all the other states (according to the present situation of commerce) defray the expenses of twenty Algerine rovers. In short, the American states, rich in the productions of nature, are poor with respect to the improvements of art. They are too strong to be conquered, and too weak to attempt conquest.

I have lately heard of a society in this country, called Free-masons, who are remarkable for inviolable secrecy. Rather than disclose a secret, they would endure extreme torture and submit to be torn in pieces. What admirable spies would these men make, if employed by their country at foreign courts! But perhaps their established reputation would render their exertions ineffectual, just as a very skillful gamester, when his talents are known, finds no body willing to play with him except for trifles. I too am possessed of a secret, but am by no means desirous of appearing to possess it. Ambition is best concealed by a show of popular humility, and secrecy rendered secure by apparent frankness.

FAREWELL.

LETTER XXI.

SOLOMON MENDEZ TO MEHEMET.

GIBRALTAR.

WITH the greatest anxiety for thy welfare and life I snatch this opportunity to inform thee, that thou must never think of returning to Algiers. If this letter should find thee in Philadelphia, how happy shall I be! The Rabbi, with whom thou had some acquaintance at Lisbon, has effected thy ruin by the blackest calumnies. How thou has offended him I know not; but I am well informed by an intelligent friend at Algiers, that he has represented thee to the regency as a Christian and a fugitive from thy country. By order of the Dey, thy lands, house, furniture and slaves (two excepted) are confiscated to the state. Thou art proclaimed a traitor; consequently if ever thou should be found within

the territories of Algiers, thy life will be for-
feited. Unhappy man!—But perhaps thy fortitude will raise thee above thy distresses.—I
sincerely hope so —

The sum, which thou did entrust to me, is
at thy disposal. None of thy bills, if thou has
yet drawn any, have been presented to me. Thy
frugality allows me to hope, that thou has not
expended the money, which was thought adequate to thy probable necessities during thy
abode in America. Thy economy, even when
there was no immediate occasion for it, was
remarkable and exemplary. It is now absolutely
necessary. If enough shall remain to render age
not altogether uncomfortable, what more can
thou require? besides thou may rely on my
assistance. In all exigencies look on me as a
warm disinterested friend. My house, my
purse, my credit, are at thy service. Can I do
less for a man, who thought me worthy of his
confidence, not only in pecuniary matters, but
even in an affair on which his life depended?

Having now administered comfort to thee
with respect to thy future prospects, I request

that thou will read the enclosed letters with becoming fortitude. Thy child they will inform thee is in heaven; and that thou art preserved from the machinations of two domestic traitors, ought to afford thee extreme happiness.

FAREWELL.

LETTER XXII.

ALGIERS.

How shall I inform thee of thy misfortunes? What language shall I adopt, which, while it reveals thy ruin, may administer consolation and inspire fortitude? Mehemet, thou art declared a traitor! The malice of thy foes is triumphant. Thy friends are struck with terror. Myself alone dared to speak in thy favor to Osman; but was commanded to be silent. "His traitorous conduct said this haughty favorite, is too evident. A letter from a Rabbi at Lisbon created suspicion, and the flight of the partner of his bed and his chief gardener has confirmed his guilt." I still had the boldness to request, that he would peruse the enclosed letters. He condescended to read them, but in the greatest hurry; then returning them, expressed himself in these very words, as well as I can remember, "Wretch! Begone. Dost thou hope to impose on my understanding by such shallow devices? After having taken with him his money and jewels, does he think, that the flight of his favorite slaves will not be attributed to the design of meeting him in some Christian country, where, after having embraced the superstition of these infidels, they will unite in reviling our laws and religion?"—Thus thy greatest misfortune being regarded as a proof of thy guilt, I was incapable of making any reply, and departed in silence.

What I have written will inform thee, that Fatima and thy chief gardener are fled. The enclosed letter, which arrived about a week ago from Spain, will doubtless give thee the particulars. Fatima's jewels and apparel remain; as for cash, no more has been supplied by me, than what was necessary for domestic uses. There remain in my hands of thy property, thirteen hundred and fifteen Johanneses, besides the above mentioned jewels, which shall be immediately paid to thy order.

I am extremely sorry to inform thee, that thou must resign all hopes of returning. Thy slaves, house, gardens and furniture, have been publicly purchased by Achmet, the tool of Osman, who, it is supposed by thy friends, will soon take possession of his villainously acquired property. How will thy friends be mortified, when they see this renegado possessed of thy abode, where taste and magnificence were united!

Mehemet! thy youth has been honorably spent. Let not fortitude desert thee in the meridian of thy faculties. Algiers has now no claim on thee. Thy child died a few weeks before the departure of his unworthy mother, and thy friends will rejoice to hear, that thou art happily situated in a country where the adoration of but one God is enjoined.

Solomon Mendez has frequently written to me concerning thee in the most friendly manner. His character is so well established, that I might safely remit thy property to him; but I shall wait till I hear from thee.

How will thy enemies exult, should they hear, that thou has yielded to desperation or melancholy!—How will thy friends rejoice, when they are informed, that philosophy has triumphed over rapacity, and that Mehemet is happier in his retirement, than Osman in the zenith of false glory!

FAREWELL.

LETTER XXIII.

ALVAREZ TO SOLYMAN.

MALAGA.

BEING informed by Maria, formerly
Fatima, who, having received baptism
according to the rites of the church, has consented to be my wife, that you are authorized
by Mehemet to superintend his business during his absence, I think it reasonable, in order
to relieve you from suspense, to inform you,
that we arrived in this port, after a very short
passage, in perfect health. As I am under no
obligation to Mehemet, no apology for my
conduct is due to him. His behavior to me, I
confess (due allowance being made for education and example) was humane and liberal.
The money therefore, which he gave as the
price of my freedom, shall be restored to him

speedily and with interest. As he has frequently acknowledged my industry and fidelity, he
will then be in my debt.

He will probably say, that I have robbed
him of Maria; but as he shall have no just reason to complain of me with respect to any part
of his property, her value also, according to the
current price of beauty at Algiers, shall be paid
to him. As for her affections, he may rest
assured, that he never possessed them. She
endured his company, because she was his
slave, and her mildness of temper prevented
her from expressing discontent.

Let it not be said, that I made use of unjus-
tifiable methods in gaining her heart. As long
their child was living, I considered her as united to Mehemet by that tie. I pitied her situation and esteemed her for her gentleness and
discretion. But on the death of the child, pity
produced affection and esteem ripened into
love. My eyes and behavior at first testified my
sentiments. She saw, and did not disapprove.
At length I ventured to disclose my passion.
She listened, and consented. A virtuous affec-

tion removed her natural timidity. Our love was mutual and ardent; the coast of Spain not distant. We ventured and succeeded; but by what methods must remain a secret. Convinced by my arguments. she is now a Christian and my wife. The liberality of some merchants supplied us with decent clothing, and their patronage will afford me the means of supporting a family by industry.

When you write to Mehemet, you may acquaint him that I retain a due sense of his mildness and forbearance. Not to be severe is meritorious, in a country where slavery is established. I am no longer his slave, and am therefore capable of being his friend. As for Maria, she does not speak of him with disrespect. She is a Christian and forgives him.

I am, Sir,

Your most obedient

Humble servant.

ALVAREZ.

LETTER XXIV.

PHILADELPHIA.

RUINED, did thou say?—No; I am pre-served. I am free and delight in the freedom of others, and am no longer either a slave or a tyrant. At once a Christian and a Pennsylvanian, I am doubly an advocate for the rights of mankind.

On the receipt of this packet, instantly dispatch the enclosed letters to the young couple. The letter to Alvarez contains a deed, which gives to him and his wife an immediate right to the half of my property, and to the remainder at my death. Supply them with a thousand dollars, in order to free them from debts, if they have contracted any, and to enable them to repair to Philadelphia. If that sum be not sufficient, supply them with more. Convinced from a perfect knowledge of the fluctuation of our councils, that the charge I undertook, exposed me to more danger in Algiers than America, I brought with me a greater sum than even thou were aware of; a part of which, since the account of my ruin, as thou called my deliverance, I have laid out in the purchase of two extensive farms; on one of which I shall reside myself; the other is the property of Alvarez and his wife. Him I shall regard as my friend and Maria shall be unto me as a daughter.

Insult not my understanding by bestowing the name of generosity on this conduct. If I can be just to this ill treated pair, my mind will be at ease, nor can I in this instance, lay claim to the merit of philosophy. At sixty the tumult of the passions ought to subside, without any assistance from philosophic resignation.

Yet I must confess, that, on the receipt of thy last letter, I was greatly shocked. A fever ensued, attended with a delirium. My extreme temperance alone preserved my life. At length the fever abated. I am restored to health and peace, and am even astonished, that my mind should have been so long the seat of unworthy passions. Was my love the result of reason? by no means; I have therefore discarded it. Was my ambition founded on justice? Alas treachery and virtue are incompatible. How am I afflicted, when I recollect, that, in all possible cases, the laws of the country, which I meant to betray, would have protected me from insult and injury. An open enemy may challenge esteem; a spy is a mean and detestable character. I have written to Solyman at Algiers, concerning a sum of money belonging to me, which is in his possession. He will remit that sum to thee on my account, which will remain in thy hands, till the arrival of Maria and her husband in Philadelphia. When my family (they are all that Mehemet can now lay claim to) shall arrive, I shall close my affairs in Africa and Europe, and establish my future tranquility on the pillars of freedom, justice, friendship and religion.

Algiers! thou, who has often beheld me, animated by glory, or incited by avarice, preparing to encounter the raging tempest and the furious battle; who has often welcomed thy returning son, adorned with trophies and loaded with spoils; who has often seen him encouraging the ardor of youth and soothing the woes of age; honored for his valor, and scarcely envied for his magnificence. Algiers, thou witness of my glory and disgrace, farewell! And thou Pennsylvania, who has promised to succor and protect the unhappy, that fly to thee for refuge, open thy arms to receive Mehemet the Algerine, who, formerly a Mahometan, and thy foe, has renounced his enmity, his country and his religion, and hopes, protected by thy laws, to enjoy, in the evening of his days, the united blessings of FREEDOM and CHRISTIANITY.

FAREWELL.

THE END.

INDEX